OXFORD PHILOSOPHICAL TEXTS

J. S. Mill

Utilitarianism

OXFORD PHILOSOPHICAL TEXTS

Series editor: John Cottingham

The Oxford Philosophical Texts series consists of authoritative teaching editions of canonical texts in the history of philosophy from the ancient world down to modern times. Each volume provides a clear, well laid out text together with a comprehensive introduction by a leading specialist, giving the student detailed critical guidance on the intellectual context of the work and the structure and philosophical importance of the main arguments. Endnotes are supplied which provide further commentary on the arguments and explain unfamiliar references and terminology, and a full bibliography and index are also included.

The series aims to build up a definitive corpus of key texts in the Western philosophical tradition, which will form a reliable and enduring resource for students and teachers alike.

PUBLISHED IN THIS SERIES:

Berkeley *A Treatise Concerning the Principles of Human Knowledge* (edited by Jonathan Dancy)
Berkeley *Three Dialogues between Hylas and Philonous* (edited by Jonathan Dancy)
Hume *An Enquiry concerning the Principles of Morals* (edited by Tom L. Beauchamp)
Leibniz *Philosophical Texts* (edited by R. S. Woolhouse and Richard Francks)
Mill *Utilitarianism* (edited by Roger Crisp)

FORTHCOMING TITLES INCLUDE:

Frege *Philosophical Writings* (edited by Anthony Kenny)
Hume *A Treatise of Human Nature* (edited by David Fate Norton and Mary J. Norton)
Kant *Groundwork for the Metaphysics of Morals* (edited by Thomas E. Hill and Arnulf Zweig)
Kant *Prolegomena to Any Future Metaphysics* (edited by Günter Zöller)
Locke *An Essay concerning Human Understanding* (edited by S. Nicholas Jolley)
Spinoza *Ethics* (edited by G. H. R. Parkinson)

J. S. MILL

Utilitarianism

EDITED BY
ROGER CRISP

Oxford · New York
OXFORD UNIVERSITY PRESS
1998

Oxford University Press, Great Clarendon Street, Oxford OX2 6DP

Oxford New York

Athens Auckland Bangkok Bogota Bombay Buenos Aires
Calcutta Cape Town Dar es Salaam Delhi Florence Hong Kong Istanbul
Karachi Kuala Lumpur Madras Madrid Melbourne Mexico City
Nairobi Paris Singapore Taipei Tokyo Toronto Warsaw
and associated companies in
Berlin Ibadan

Oxford is a trade mark of Oxford University Press

Published in the United States
by Oxford University Press Inc., New York

British Library Cataloguing in Publication Data
Data available

Library of Congress Cataloging in Publication Data
Mill, John Stuart, 1806–1873.
Utilitarianism/J.S. Mill; edited by Roger Crisp.
(Oxford philosophical texts)
Includes bibliographical references (p.   ) and index.
1. Utilitarianism.   I. Crisp, Roger, 1961–   .   II. Title.
III. Series.
B1603.U873M54   1998 171'.5—dc21 97-31037
ISBN 0-19-875162-1
ISBN 0-19-875163-X (Pbk.)

1 3 5 7 9 10 8 6 4 2

Typeset by Best-set Typesetter Ltd., Hong Kong
Printed in Great Britain
on acid-free paper by
Bookcraft (Bath) Ltd
Midsomer Norton, Somerset

Acknowledgements

I edited this Oxford Philosophical Text shortly after completing *Mill on Utilitarianism* for Routledge. The two works are clearly related, so the thanks offered to colleagues and students in that earlier work must be reiterated here. In addition, I am grateful to Catherine Audard for showing me a draft of her forthcoming annotated French edition of *Utilitarianism*, to John Cottingham for comments on a draft of the introduction and notes, to Jonathan Dancy for discussion of the footnote to 2.19, and to Elijah Millgram for comments on a draft of the notes. I must also acknowledge my debt to Geraint Williams's notes to his Everyman edition (London, 1993). I have been greatly assisted by grants of sabbatical leave from the Principal and Fellows of St Anne's College, the British Academy, and the University of Oxford. Finally, thanks are due to Dunedin Public Library for its donation in 1971 to the University of Oxford of a copy of the fourth edition of *Utilitarianism*, which the University had previously lacked.

Contents

PART 1

Introductory Material

How to Use this Book

This book contains the text of John Stuart Mill's *Utilitarianism*. The text follows an Editor's Introduction and an Analysis of the text, and is itself followed by Notes, a Bibliography, and an Index.

The Introduction is aimed particularly at those new to Mill and even to moral philosophy, but it contains material which will be of interest to more advanced readers. It begins by explaining Mill's main project, and then outlines the utilitarian theory of ethics. After a brief biographical account of Mill's ethics, the remainder of the Introduction provides an interpretation of the main lines of argument in *Utilitarianism* and ends with some problems for utilitarian theories.

Mill's text is not long, and it is written in his characteristic straightforward style. Nevertheless, it is more complex than it first appears. It moves swiftly from point to point, and often relies on a reader's understanding of philosophy or literature. It can, however, be read profitably without any guidance, and is best so read by anyone new to it. Reading the Introduction first may make it harder for the novice to make up their own mind about how Mill is to be interpreted. If this is too much like being thrown in at the deep end, then note that the first section of the Introduction is the most important. It would be advisable to use the Analysis of the text even on a first reading, since this will allow the reader to see at once the main structure of Mill's arguments.

The Notes are intended to provide further elucidation of the argument, cross-references, background information, and criticism. The serious student will want to read most or all of the Notes, paragraph by paragraph, while reading the text (though, as suggested above, this should not be done on a first reading). Such a person should ensure that the Note on References and Abbreviations is read and understood before using the Notes. The Notes will also be useful for dipping into when a passage is found puzzling.

There is some suggested Further Reading at the end of the Introduction. Full details of all books not by Mill referred to in the Introduction and Notes can be found in the Bibliography, those of books by Mill in the Note on References and Abbreviations. The Index can be used for research into specific topics.

A Note on References and Abbreviations

References to *Utilitarianism* are to chapter, paragraph, and (sometimes) line. Thus '4.3.5–6' refers to the fifth and sixth lines of the third paragraph of the fourth chapter. Other references to the works of Mill are abbreviated, the numbers referring to the volume and page of the *Collected Works* (ed. John Robson, 33 vols., Toronto, 1961–91). Thus '*S* 8.943' refers to page 943 of the text of *A System of Logic* in the eighth volume of the *Collected Works*. The abbreviations used are as follows:

A	*Autobiography*, 1873.	O	'On the Words Productive and
AC	*Auguste Comte and Positivism*,		Unproductive', 1844.
	1865.	*P*	*Principles of Political Economy*,
AP	*James Mill's Analysis of the*		1848.
	Phenomena of the Human Mind,	PL	'Periodical Literature:
	1869.		Edinburgh Review', 1824.
B	'Bentham', 1838.	R	'Remarks on Bentham's
BH	'Brodie's History of the British		Philosophy', 1833.
	Empire', 1824.	*RJ*	*Jeremy Bentham's Rationale of*
BP	'Bain's Psychology', 1859.		*Judicial Evidence*, 1827.
C	*Considerations on Representative*	*S*	*A System of Logic Ratiocinative*
	Government, 1861.		*and Inductive*, 1843.
CC	'Cooperation: Closing Speech',	SA	'Spirit of the Age, II', 1831.
	1825.	SD	'Sedgwick's Discourse', 1833.
D	*Diary*, 1854.	*SW*	*The Subjection of Women*, 1869.
E	*An Examination of Sir*	T	'Theism', 1874.
	William Hamilton's Philosophy,	TG	'The Gorgias', 1834.
	1865.	TL	'Thornton on Labour and its
EG	'Effects of Gambling', 1823.		Claims', 1869.
G	'Grote's Plato', 1866.	TS	'Taylor's Statesman', 1837.
L	*On Liberty*, 1859.	UR	'Utility of Religion', 1874.
N	'Nature', 1874.	W	'Whewell's Moral Philosophy',
NQ	'The Negro Question', 1850.		1852.

Mill's letters are again referred to using references to the Toronto edition. Details of works by other authors will be found in the Bibliography.

Editor's Introduction

1. What Questions is Mill Trying to Answer?

> From the dawn of philosophy, the question concerning the *summum bonum*, or, what is the same thing, concerning the foundation of morality, has been accounted the main problem in speculative thought, has occupied the most gifted intellects, and divided them into sects and schools, carrying on a vigorous warfare against one another. And after more than two thousand years the same discussions continue . . .
>
> (*Utilitarianism* 1.1)

Philosophy dawned in Athens in the fifth century BC, when Socrates asked the young men who came to converse with him the question, 'How should one live?' Answering this question itself involved answering three further questions. What is happiness? What is the morally right way to live or to act? And what is the relation between happiness and morality? These are the three central questions addressed by Mill in *Utilitarianism*. His answers are the following. First, happiness is pleasure. Secondly, the right way to act is to produce the greatest amount of happiness overall. Thirdly, in a properly constituted world, the individual's happiness will be found in doing what is morally right.

Many students come to moral philosophy for the first time through Mill's *Utilitarianism*. It is easy for those who have been brought up on a diet of science and social science, that is, disciplines concerned with how the world *is*, to miss the remarkable fact that Mill is writing not primarily about how the world is, but about how it *should* be. He is not claiming that individual agents do in fact act so as to produce the greatest happiness, rather that this is what they ought to do. And when students realize this, their first reaction is often one of incredulity, for surely we all know that there is no right answer to questions such as 'What is happiness?' or 'What is it right to do?'? It is up to each person to decide for themselves.

This kind of 'subjectivism' about ethics is pervasive, but it does not go very deep. Despite the temptations of scepticism, nearly everyone will in fact commiserate with a friend who has suffered a personal disaster, or criticize someone who has gone beyond the moral pale. Practices such as these are incoherent unless the kinds of question Socrates and Mill tried to answer make sense.

2. What are the Alternatives to Utilitarianism?

We can be afraid, e.g., or be confident, or have appetites, or get angry, or feel pity, in general have pleasure or pain, both too much and too little, and in both ways not well; but [having these feelings] at the right times, about the right things, towards the right people, for the right end, and in the right way, is the intermediate and best condition, and this is proper to virtue.

(Aristotle *c*.330 BC / 1985: 1106^{b}18–23)

There is . . . only one categorical imperative. It is: Act only according to that maxim by which you can at the same time will that it should become a universal law.

(Kant 1785 / 1995: 38)

Before going on to discuss Mill's own view in detail, it will be worth describing briefly the views of the philosophers who have become his two main opponents in modern ethics: Aristotle and Immanuel Kant.

Aristotle was a pupil of Plato, himself a pupil of Socrates, and in his ethical writings he continued the Socratic agenda. Aristotle's view was that understanding happiness required attention to human nature. What makes human beings what they are is their capacity to reason. Living the good life will be living the good human life, and that, Aristotle argued, would involve exercising the capacity for reason *well*, that is, 'in accordance with excellence'. 'Excellence', for Aristotle, is roughly equivalent to 'virtue', so it turns out that happiness consists in the exercise of one's capacity for virtue. The happy life is the life of generosity, even temper, justice, and so on.

Through his answer to the question of what happiness is, Aristotle manages to supply answers also to the questions concerning morality, and the relation between happiness and morality, for the happy life just is the moral life. Many contemporary thinkers have been profoundly influenced by various aspects of this Aristotelian position. These philosophers are likely to disagree with Mill's view that happiness consists in pleasure, and more especially with his notion that morality consists in maximizing overall pleasure. Rather, they will suggest, morality is founded on the *virtues*. Modern virtue ethics, then, is one important alternative to utilitarianism.

Immanuel Kant was a German philosopher of the eighteenth century. Like Aristotle, he believed that ethics or morality should be, in some sense, grounded on human rationality. But for him rationality was a much more abstract affair. Rather than tie rationality to the virtues of a fourth century BC Athenian, Kant attempted to construct a universal morality based on pure reason. The 'moral law', as he called it, while it would *support* many rules against murder, theft, and so on, would not at its most foundational level refer to such rules, for that would be to make it too specific to count as a viable law of reason. Kant's view was that moral action consisted in acting in accordance with a principle which one could will as a universal law of nature (this is his so-called 'categorical imperative').

Here is an example of how this rather abstract categorical imperative might support some more specific moral rule. Imagine that I am broke, and need some money for my dinner. I ask you for a loan, promising you that I shall pay you back tomorrow, but knowing that I shall be unable to do so. According to Kant, the categorical imperative supports a rule that speaks against my action, for I could not will it to be a universal law of nature that anyone who can obtain something from another through deception do so. In such a world communication would break down to the point where promising became impossible. What grounds Kant's view, partly anyway, is the appeal of the idea that it is unfair for a person to allow exceptions in their own case to moral rules which they would themselves wish society to be governed by.

Kant's view of morality, then, is quite different from those of both Aristotle and Mill. Rather than basing it on the virtues, or on the maximization of happiness, Kant sees morality as constituted by certain *rules*, requiring the keeping of promises and so on, these rules themselves being based on abstract rationality through the categorical imperative. There is some debate about whether Kant's axioms are in fact inconsistent with utilitarianism. Mill himself argues that they are not (1.4). But certainly many moral philosophers today believe that Kantian morality constitutes a second important alternative to utilitarianism.

3. John Stuart Mill and Utilitarianism

[I]n an age of transition in opinions, there may be somewhat both of interest and of benefit in noting the successive phases of any mind which was always pressing forward.

(A 1.5)

John Stuart Mill was born in 1806. His father, James Mill, was also a utilitarian philosopher, and a strong believer in the importance of education. In his autobiography, John Stuart tells us: 'I have no remembrance of the time when I began to learn Greek. I have been told that it was when I was three years old' (*A* 1.9). Mill was educated at home. Indeed he learned his Latin and Greek in the same room as his father, interrupting the latter's work on a substantial history of India in order to ask him questions of vocabulary. He became extremely well read, but the intensity of his learning took its toll, and at the age of 20 he suffered a nervous breakdown. Mill's father had offered him little poetry, but it was poetry, particularly that of Wordsworth, on which Mill relied during his recovery. From this time on, he began to seek insight from thinkers who had little in common with his father or with the utilitarian philosopher Jeremy Bentham (1748–1832), who had also been closely implicated in his upbringing.

But Mill did not abandon his background. Rather he sought to bring together the points of view of his father and Bentham with those of Thomas Carlyle (1795–1881), Auguste Comte (1798–1857), and others. Once he had been exposed to Bentham's utilitarianism, he never deserted it: 'It gave unity to my conceptions of things. I now had opinions; a creed, a doctrine, a philosophy; in one among all the best senses of the word, a religion; the inculcation and diffusion of which could be made the principal outward purpose of a life' (*A* 1.69).

Utilitarianism, then, was the cornerstone of Mill's writings. But he retained other important principles bequeathed to him by his father and Bentham. Most importantly, he was an *empiricist*, who believed that knowledge is based on experience through the senses, and an *associationist*, who claimed that the mind's workings depend on law-governed associations of ideas with one another.

Mill's education had kept him apart from society. His love life was to do the same. In 1830, he began a love affair with a married woman, Harriet Taylor, which continued until Harriet's death in 1858 (the couple married in 1851, after the death of Harriet's first husband in 1849). Mill supported himself through a successful career with the East India Company, a private organization which ran India on behalf of the British Government. But he had plenty of time for intellectual activity. His written output was vast, running to nearly forty large volumes in the *Collected Works*. His last words, to his stepdaughter in 1873, were apt: 'You know that I have done my work.'

Before discussing some of the specific issues Mill raises in *Utilitarianism*, let me first offer an outline of its structure (the detail is filled in by the textual analysis at the close of this Introduction). In chapter 1, Mill discusses the state and methods of moral philosophy. Some of his central claims are related to his proof of utilitarianism in chapter 4, so I shall discuss these issues together in Section 7 below. In chapter 2, Mill outlines his view of happiness (to be discussed in my next Section) and his understanding of utilitarianism (see my Sections 5 and 6). In chapter 3, on 'sanctions', he discusses the questions of moral motivation and the relation of happiness to morality (see my Section 8). The longest chapter in *Utilitarianism* is on justice, and to that I shall devote Section 9.

4. Happiness

> By happiness is intended pleasure, and the absence of pain; by unhappiness, pain, and the privation of pleasure.
>
> (2.2)

We have already noted that providing an account of happiness was seen by the ancients as the central component of an answer to the question of how to live. This important fact has been often ignored in more recent philosophy. It has been assumed that happiness, and related notions such as well-being, welfare, or self-interest, belong squarely within utilitarian territory, and need not be taken seriously by non-utilitarian philosophers.

The ancients were right. Consider, for example, virtue ethics and Kantian ethics. First, most forms of modern virtue ethics will include benevolence, beneficence, or kindness in their lists of virtues, and most versions of Kantian ethics will involve principles requiring one to benefit others in various ways. Beneficence is impossible, however, unless one has some idea of what in fact will benefit someone else, and that will require an account of happiness or welfare. Secondly, we should consider seriously deficient an ethics which contains no answer to the question of the relation between morality and the happiness of the moral agent.

Mill's conception of happiness, then, is only one among many. It is important to note that this conception is quite independent from his utilitarianism as a whole. According to utilitarianism, my moral duty is to maximize happiness. That position is separable from any particular view of what happiness is. Thus, one can accept Mill's view of happiness, and deny utilitarianism; or deny his view of happiness, but accept utilitarianism. Indeed, one can see happiness as independent from morality altogether. An egoist, who believes that the only reasons for action anyone has are self-interested, could accept the main thrust of Mill's conception of happiness. *Moral* objections to Mill's theory of happiness are therefore misplaced.

Mill's utilitarian forbears, as we have seen, were both empiricists and associationists, that is, they placed emphasis on sense experience both as a source of knowledge and as the key to understanding the mind. It was natural for them, therefore, to offer accounts of happiness—of what makes life worth living—in terms of pleasurable mental states. The view that happiness consists in pleasure is known as *hedonism* (*hēdonē* is the ancient Greek word for 'pleasure').

The most sophisticated development of hedonism before Mill was in the work of Jeremy Bentham, especially his *Principles of Morals and Legislation*. Bentham claimed that pleasure was a kind of sensation, common to all those experiences described as enjoyable or as contributing to the value of a life to the person living it. Likewise, 'pain' refers to all those experiences, including both physical pain and mental suffering of all kinds, which people find objectionable.

The best life for a person, Bentham suggests, will consist in the greatest *balance* of pleasure over pain. It can therefore be worth undergoing certain pains—such as those of a medical operation—in order to produce the greatest balance of pleasure over pain in the long run. Because, according to Bentham, all pleasures and all pains are structurally similar sensations, it should be possible to construct a *felicific calculus*, in order to measure the value of various courses of action. The value of the several pleasures and pains possible through acting in a particular way can be calculated, and then multiplied by the probability of the action's in fact having that upshot. This gives the so-called 'expected utility' of the action in question.

There is, of course, a serious question about whether such calculations are possible. But there is a yet deeper problem, arising out of the very assumptions on which this model of calculation is based. Let me employ an admittedly fanciful philosophical 'thought experiment'. Imagine that you are a soul, waiting to be allocated a life. You are offered either the life of the composer, Joseph Haydn, or that of an oyster. Haydn's life is quite long, involving great success and enjoyment. The life of the oyster consists only in the most simple and primitive pleasurable experience possible. Of course, you ask for the life of Haydn; but you are then told that the life of the oyster can be as long as you like—millions of years, if you so desire.

According to Bentham's view, since all pleasures are measurable on a single scale, there must come a point at which the oyster life becomes more worthy of choice than that of the composer. Many people will feel unhappy about this implication, thinking that what one would lose by not choosing Haydn's life could never be compensated for by any number of years of primitive pleasure.

Mill's famous distinction between quality and quantity of pleasure can be seen as an attempt to spell out this point. Mill followed Bentham in being a hedonist. Pleasurable experience is the only thing worth having, and it is good because of its pleasurableness. Bentham had employed two main criteria for measuring the value of any pleasurable experience: the duration of the experience and the intensity of the pleasure. Mill added to this the idea that the very *nature* of the pleasure in question was important: 'It is quite compatible with the principle of utility to recognize the fact, that some *kinds* of pleasure are more desirable and more valuable than others' (2.4).

Mill would suggest that pleasures of the kind experienced by Haydn are usually more intense and long-lasting than the 'lower' pleasures. But greater intensity and duration alone cannot make a pleasure higher than another. When comparing two pleasures,

[i]f one of the two is, by those who are competently acquainted with both, placed so far above the other that they prefer it . . . we are justified in ascribing to the preferred enjoyment a superiority in quality, so far outweighing quantity as to render it, in comparison, of small account. (2.5)

Mill can explain, then, why it is that many people would prefer, in my thought experiment, the life of Haydn to that of the oyster. The intellectual pleasures of writing a great symphony, say, are such that no amount of mere physical enjoyment could counterbalance them.

Since Mill first made this claim, he has often been charged with denying hedonism. The argument goes as follows. If he remains a hedonist, then he must accept that the only value is pleasantness, and, if this is the case, then adding pleasantness to one side of the scale must eventually lead it to tip. The oyster life, in other words, must, if one is a hedonist, eventually become more valuable than that of Haydn. If, however, Mill would wish to claim that the life of Haydn remains more valuable *however much* pleasantness is added to the other pan of the scale, then he must be suggesting that something other than pleasantness is valuable, and so be denying hedonism.

This common argument against Mill assumes that Benthamite hedonism is the only version available, but that is exactly what Mill wishes to deny. According to Bentham, the value of a pleasure depends only on its intensity and duration. Like Bentham, Mill believes that pleasantness is the only 'good-making' property. But how valuable a pleasure is depends not only on its duration, but on its nature. Mill can thus avoid the objection, remaining a hedonist of a kind quite different from Bentham.

There is nevertheless something to the criticism of Mill, in that there might appear to be an explanatory gap in his account. The problem is that the kinds of properties to which he refers when he speaks of the nature of the higher pleasures seem themselves to be such that they might themselves be good-making. Length or intensity, on their own, do not add value. Indeed, in the case of pains, they can detract from value. Mill speaks, for example, of the *nobility* of higher pleasures as explaining their greater value, but if nobility can add value when it is a property itself of pleasurableness, why can it not add value on its own? Why cannot an experience of great nobility, even if it is not enjoyed, still be valuable? And if it is enjoyed, why should we think that its value is exhausted by its contribution to pleasurableness? Further, and perhaps most importantly, why should nobility add to *pleasurableness* at all? Indeed, how could it? What notion of pleasure is Mill working with?

Let me put those questions aside, for there remains yet another problem for hedonism in general. Hedonism is most straightforwardly understood as the claim that certain *experiences*—themselves taken to be mental states—are valuable (that is, pleasurable) experiences. Now consider the following thought experiment. Imagine that I am able to predict the quantity and quality of the pleasures and pains you will experience over the rest of your life. I then offer you a choice: either you can live out the rest of your life in the ordinary way; or you can be plugged into my experience machine. This machine will give you experiences which are indistinguishable from genuine experiences. You will still be able to make choices while on the machine, since it is programmed to allow this. The machine life has one special attraction: it will contain a slightly greater balance of pleasure over pain than will your life off the machine, in the 'real world'. Many people believe that plugging into the machine will not in fact improve your life. Anyone who believes that must deny the straightforward version of hedonism, according to which the value of a life depends solely on the degree of overall pleasurableness of the mental states experienced in that life.

As we saw in the discussion of quality of pleasure, Mill can be seen as moving in a direction away from hedonism, though he never finally abandoned it, for he comes very close to giving properties such as nobility an independent, good-making role. Similarly, it may be that his hedonism itself can be understood to place a special value on the *genuine* experience of certain activities. Mill himself does not, of course, address these questions directly, but it is hard to accept that he himself would have thought preferable the life on the experience machine.

5. Forms of Utilitarianism

> The creed which accepts as the foundation of morals, Utility, or the Greatest Happiness Principle, holds that actions are right in proportion as they tend to promote happiness, wrong as they tend to produce the reverse of happiness.
>
> (2.2)

We have already said something of virtue ethics and Kantian ethics, two alternatives to utilitarianism. Now it is time for us to consider utilitarianism itself, and in particular the form of it to which Mill subscribed. It might appear as if what Mill says here is quite straightforward, and, indeed, it is sometimes said that one of the main attractions of utilitarianism is its simplicity. But utilitarianism is in fact far from simple.

First, we must consider the fact that moral theories can *focus* on different objects. A moral theory, for example, may concern a person's character, their motives, or their life as a whole. Most commonly, moral theories focus on *actions*, as does Mill himself. It is important to notice that a focus on actions does not prevent one's referring to some other notion in describing which actions are right, or what makes actions right. Consider, for example, motive utilitarianism. This view is not usually offered as the view that one should have those motives that are most productive of overall happiness or welfare. Rather, it states that one should perform those actions which would be performed by someone with motives most productive of overall happiness. It is a view about actions.

One component of any utilitarian theory is likely to be *welfarism*. This is the view that the only good thing in the world is happiness or welfare, usually of sentient beings (so both Bentham and Mill were concerned to bring non-human animals beneath the moral umbrella). There is no independent good in, for example, justice or equality, or in the beauty of works of art or landscapes. All that matters, morally, is how well the lives of sentient beings go for them.

Utilitarianism is often described as a *consequentialist* theory, and the difference between consequentialism and non-consequentialism is in turn outlined roughly as follows. A non-consequentialist theory, such as Kantian ethics, will claim that certain actions are just wrong *in themselves*, and not wrong because of their consequences for happiness or anything else. But consequentialist theories make the rightness of actions depend on their consequences. Kantian ethics may claim that murder is wrong in itself, while utilitarianism will claim that it is wrong only because of its consequences (the decrease in overall happiness brought about by the absence of the person killed, by the grief, distress, anxiety caused to others, and so on).

The consequentialist/non-consequentialist distinction so described, however, is confused. For utilitarianism itself can be read as claiming that certain actions are wrong in themselves, namely, those that fail to maximize happiness. A recent alternative to this distinction which scholars have attempted to use is the so-called *agent-relative/agent-neutral* distinction. Agent-neutral theories give to each agent the same aims (e.g. that utility be maximized), whereas agent-relative theories, such as many forms of Kantianism, give different aims to each agent (e.g. that *your own* children be cared for). Logically, however, a utilitarian can insist that *your* aim should be that *you* maximize utility. This theory would, of course, be practically equivalent to an agent-neutral theory, but practical equivalence is not logical equivalence (it might be argued that utilitarianism, virtue ethics, and Kantianism are all practically equivalent).

So rather than looking for some philosophical distinction to capture the essence of utilitarianism, it is wiser to attempt a description of exactly what the content of utilitarianism itself is. Mill's view we may call *act utilitarianism*, and it appears to state that the right action in any circumstance is that which produces the greatest overall balance of pleasure over pain. This view, however, has some odd consequences. Imagine that a certain doctor is faced with the following situation. Her patient is suffering from a condition for which there are two treatments, A and B. A will restore the patient to full health, while B will produce only partial health. It might seem clear that the doctor should choose A. But consider the following important fact: A has only a 1 per cent chance of success, and if it fails the patient will die, while *B* is pretty well guaranteed to succeed. Now imagine that the doctor chooses *A*, and by chance it is successful. According to act utilitarianism as we have understood it so far, she seems to have done the right thing. And, even more surprisingly, had she chosen *B*, this would have been the wrong thing (though of course no one could have known).

For reasons such as this, and so as to provide a workable morality, most utilitarians do not express their view in terms of the *actual* but rather the *expected* outcomes of actions. The expected outcome of an action is calculated by multiplying the value of the outcome by the probability of its occurring. Since, in our example, the probability of success in the case of *A* was so low, the expected value of the outcome would also have been low.

The actual/expected distinction can be seen as a distinction between two kinds of rightness, objective and subjective. From the objective point of view, a utilitarian might claim, the right action is the one that in fact maximizes happiness; while from the subjective point of view, the point of view of the agent, the right action is the one that maximizes expected happiness. If the utilitarian is ready to accept that there are both kinds of rightness, then they do not have to choose between an actual and an expected version of their theory. The actual version operates at the objective level, the expected at the subjective. It is perhaps best to understand Mill as such a utilitarian, since at times he suggests that the morality of an action depends on its *foreseeable* consequences (see e.g. the footnote to 2.19).

Allowing Mill to accept the expected version of act utilitarianism as an account of subjective rightness enables him to avoid a serious objection to the actual version as a guide to action, namely, that consequences stretch indefinitely into the future, so that we can never know which action is the right one. For, according to probabilistic utilitarianism, unknown probabilities can be removed from the calculation of expected utility and hence from the account of rightness itself.

So far, then, we have discussed the issues of focus, and the actual/ expected distinction (and the related objective/subjective distinction). The next question to consider in analysing any form of utilitarianism is exactly what it requires us to maximize, for the requirement to maximize happiness (or expected happiness) can be understood in at least two ways. According to the *total* version of act utilitarianism, the right action is that which produces the greatest total balance of happiness over unhappiness. According to the *average* version, the right action is that which produces the greatest average balance.

These theories might appear to be practically equivalent, and, in a fixed population, indeed they are. Maximizing the total will be the same as maximizing the average, and vice versa. But differences emerge when one considers the implications of utilitarianism for future generations. Here, the average view leads to the absurd conclusion that I should not have a child, even if its life will be very happy and there will no overall detrimental effect arising from its existence, if its happiness will be lower than the existing average. But the total view also runs into problems, most famously with what Derek Parfit has called the 'Repugnant Conclusion'. This conclusion is that if a population of people with lives barely worth living is large enough, it is preferable to a smaller—but perhaps extremely large—population of people with very happy lives.

Mill offers us the total view. Interestingly, his distinction between higher and lower pleasures may enable him to sidestep the Repugnant Conclusion, for he might argue that the components of happiness which will be sacrificed in order to produce large numbers of people with lives barely worth living will not be compensated for by the mere increase in duration of pleasurable experience. This answer, of course, is structurally similar to the answer I suggested Mill might make to the Haydn/oyster problem.

Mill is not always interpreted as an act utilitarian, but sometimes as a *rule utilitarian*. One of the problems with act utilitarianism is that it seems to have counter-intuitive implications, implications which go against common sense. We shall discuss some of these cases below, particularly in the section on justice. One implication of act utilitarianism, for example, is that you should break a promise to your dearest friend, if doing so will increase the level of overall happiness by only a very small amount. Many people believe that a theory which has these implications cannot be correct.

Rule utilitarianism avoids many of these implications. Like act utilitarianism, its focus is actions. But unlike act utilitarianism, which is a *direct* theory, in that the rightness and wrongness of acts depends directly on whether they fit with the maximizing principle, rule utilitarianism is an *indirect* theory, since rightness and wrongness depend on rules, the justification for which itself rests on the utilitarian principle. Thus, rule utilitarianism is the view that the right action is that which is in accord with that set of rules which, if generally or universally accepted, would maximize utility.

Rule utilitarianism avoids not only the counter-intuitive moral implications of act utilitarianism, but also the stringency of act utilitarianism. Act utilitarianism is a very demanding moral view, since it counts equally the interests of each being. Other things being equal, a certain pleasure or pain should matter to me equally, whether it is to be experienced by me, a friend or a relative of mine, or a complete stranger. In our world, this appears to result in act utilitarianism's becoming very demanding. The usual example offered is that of famine relief. By surrendering all of your spare time and most of your money to famine relief, you will save many lives and prevent much suffering. Act utilitarians often suggest here that their view requires only what human beings can deliver, and that there are limits to the human will or to human psychology. But the sense of 'can' they require is obscure, since in any ordinary sense I can give up my job and spend my life campaigning for Oxfam. What seems particularly objectionable, unfair even, about the demands made by act utilitarianism, is that so much is required of me because others are not making a contribution. Why should the moral demands on me fluctuate because other people are not complying with morality? Again, rule utilitarianism respects our intuitions here, since its code is 'ideal', based on a description of an imaginary world in which most people comply with moral demands. In that world, it can be argued, it would maximize happiness if each person surrendered, say, 5 per cent of their income to development programmes.

What is the evidence for Mill's being a rule rather than an act utilitarian? One piece of alleged evidence comes from the passage in 2.2 quoted at the head of this section. Note that Mill there speaks of the 'tendencies' of actions to promote happiness or unhappiness. It is argued that an *individual* act cannot have a tendency, but that this is possible only for a *class* of acts.

This evidence, however, is far from conclusive. First, in ordinary English, an individual item can have a tendency. A ship, for example, can be said to have a tendency to starboard. Secondly, this individualistic usage was standard in the utilitarian tradition. Indeed, Mill makes use of it himself in a letter of 1872 to John Venn:

> I agree with you that the right way of testing actions by their consequences, is to test them by the natural consequences of the particular action, and not by those which would follow if every one did the same. But, for the most part, the consideration of what would happen if every one did the same, is the only means we have of discovering the tendency of the act in the particular case. (17.1881)

This passage is particularly interesting for our purposes. It employs 'tendency' in an individualistic way, and it demonstrates a clear commitment to act utilitarianism. But it shows that Mill thought that we should often *think* in a rule utilitarian way. How a commitment to a non-act-utilitarian way of thinking is not a commitment to act utilitarianism I shall demonstrate in the following section.

Several other passages from *Utilitarianism* have been adduced as evidence for an ascription of rule utilitarianism to Mill, one particularly important passage being 2.19. But I shall leave detailed discussion of these to the footnotes, in the hope that the letter to Venn is sufficient for the present to allay any doubt about the traditional act utilitarian interpretation of Mill.

6. Levels of Moral Thinking

> It is a strange notion that the acknowledgment of a first principle is inconsistent with the admission of secondary ones. To inform a traveller respecting the place of his ultimate destination, is not to forbid the use of landmarks and direction-posts on the way.
>
> (2.24)

Mill claims that the right act is that which maximizes the overall balance of happiness over unhappiness. It is tempting to think that he must therefore be suggesting that human beings should always *try* to bring about this result when they act. But this would be to ignore another important distinction between different types of utilitarianism. This distinction is unfortunately often confused with that between act and rule utilitarianism. But, as I shall show below, a utilitarian who advocates the use of rules in practice can still be an act utilitarian.

Mill's act utilitarian theory concerns what he calls the 'criterion' of right action (1.1), that is, what makes actions right, not how we should go about acting. It does not follow from the claim that what makes actions right is their maximizing happiness that this should be the conscious goal of moral agents every time they act.

The gap between a theory of the criterion of morality and a theory of decision-making is not opened up by utilitarianism alone. Consider virtue ethics. According to that view, the right action is that which is done virtuously. But, often, trying to act virtuously will be exactly what a virtuous person would not do. When I see a beggar, I reach immediately into my pocket because I am generous and want to help, not so that I can act virtuously. Trying to act virtuously would be morally self-defeating in these circumstances.

A similar kind of self-defeat emerges in the case of act utilitarianism. Imagine what a society would be like in which the only moral principle was the act utilitarian principle. The people in this society would have no qualms about killing or deceiving others. They would have no deep personal relationships, in the sense in which such relationships require one to give special weight to the interests of the person with whom one has the relationship.

Myself, I doubt whether such a society is in fact a possible one for human beings, but we can sidestep this question by noting a serious problem with a theory which advocates constant and single-minded employment of the utilitarian principle. According to such a theory, every action is justified only if it maximizes happiness. Using the utilitarian principle is itself an action in the relevant sense, so the position here must be that use of the act utilitarian principle will itself maximize happiness. But it appears unlikely that, in practice, it would.

Practising act utilitarians would almost certainly have to spend vast amounts of time calculating the pleasures and pains of the various courses of action open to them, and the probabilities related to each. Indeed, constantly practising act utilitarianism would mean constantly calculating. There would have to be rules about when to stop calculating and get on with acting, and it is a short step from such rules to the rules of common-sense morality, according to which acts such as killing or deceiving are wrong. As Mill says: 'mankind must by this time have acquired positive beliefs as to the effects of some actions on their happiness; and the beliefs which have thus come down are the rules of morality for the multitude, and for the philosopher until he has succeeded in finding better' (2.24).

Mill believes that 'customary morality'—that set of fairly specific injunctions which most of us have been brought up to accept and which govern our lives to a greater or lesser degree—has emerged gradually, 'due to the tacit influence of a standard not recognised' (1.4). That standard, of course, is the utilitarian one. Mill believes that utilitarianism is the only reasonable standard of morals, and, though there have been many factors distorting the moral vision of humanity, there has nevertheless been an almost unconscious convergence in practice on moral principles grounded on the maximization of happiness. These customary rules are not themselves, then, foundational. They are *aids* to the maximization of happiness in practice, saving time and relying on the wisdom of the ages concerning the effects that certain types of action have on happiness as a whole. That is why Mill compares them to the Nautical Almanack. But one should beware of thinking of customary morality as consisting in mere 'rules of thumb'. If a sailor can see his port on the horizon, he will cast aside his Almanack. But customary morality is not like that. Going against customary morality may engender deep feelings of guilt or compunction.

Mill does not believe, however, that utilitarianism should be confined to the philosopher's study. The morality we live by, day by day, should also include the act utilitarian principle of entirely impartial benevolence. When should it be used? '[O]nly in . . . cases of conflict between secondary principles is it requisite that first principles should be appealed to' (2.25). A friend is in hospital, and you have promised to visit that afternoon; but an urgent meeting of the local branch of Oxfam has been called to discuss how to respond to an emergency in the developing world, and you are a key member of the committee. Here, you should employ the act utilitarian principle to decide what to do.

So morality should, according to Mill, include levels of both non-utilitarian and utilitarian thinking. Mill does admit that the act utilitarian principle does not *feel* the same to us now as does, for example, the moral requirement of loyalty to a friend. But he believes that education and the opinion of society should be harnessed so that 'a direct impulse to promote the general good may be in every individual one of the habitual motives of action, and the sentiments connected therewith may fill a large and prominent place in every human being's sentient existence' (2.18).

Mill himself engages in moral discourse at several levels. His writings show that he was ready to use the ordinary moral concepts of customary morality much as anyone else. But he would also be prepared to use act utilitarian thinking in practice. Finally, he spoke at the philosophical level, beyond the everyday, of the criterion of morality itself. This philosophical discourse includes at its heart, of course, the text of *Utilitarianism* itself. The existence of the philosophical level allows Mill to avoid the charge that he conservatively accepts customary morality except where it contains an internal conflict. This would anyway be an odd charge against Mill, who believed that much of customary morality was founded on relations of domination and oppression. As he says, 'that the received code of ethics is by no means of divine right; and that mankind have still much to learn as to the effects of actions on the general happiness, I admit, or rather, earnestly maintain' (2.24). Much of Mill's own thought was directed at reflection upon, and suggestions for the improvement of, customary morality in important spheres of human life, such as the relations between the sexes, the liberty of the individual, or the distribution of property.

Mill advocates different levels of moral thinking. When the details of his scheme are made explicit, an obvious problem emerges: how are these different levels supposed to exist side by side? Consider, first, customary morality. It contains many principles forbidding various actions, such as murder, lying, betraying, and so on. Our commitment to these principles, as Mill fully realizes, is not merely 'intellectual'. They are not, as I have already suggested, mere rules of thumb. Imagine some case, such as the 'hospital/Oxfam' example I described, in which loyalty to a friend is in conflict with another customary moral principle. It is just not psychologically possible to distance oneself entirely from that loyalty, and the motivations that commitments such as friendships bring with them, and indeed largely consist in.

Customary moral dispositions pose a twofold problem in Mill's scheme. First, there is the question of how one is meant to distance oneself from them so as to adhere to an act utilitarian principle which Mill himself admits is not at present based on any strong sentiment. Secondly, if one can so distance oneself, the question arises whether act utilitarianism will not succeed in undermining these dispositions. Is not a proper friendship a relationship one will not be prepared to abandon merely for an increase in overall happiness?

The first response Mill might make to these charges is that, since he himself is fairly adept at shifting from one level of moral discourse to another, there is no reason why anybody else should find it difficult. Of course, at present, there is a lack of motivational underpinning for act utilitarianism. But this is something that Mill himself believes should be remedied, so it cannot serve well as the basis for any objection against the method of moral thinking he is advocating. Mill might then go on to admit that there is something in the charge of incoherence. He is advocating that we use customary morality as a guide to action because of our own individual failings: we do not have the time to calculate pleasures and pains, and we lack wisdom concerning the effects of various kinds of action upon human happiness. His multi-level utilitarianism is an attempt to deal with human beings as they are, and is thus bound to be something of a messy compromise between accepting their limits and attempting to extend their capacities. Ultimately, of course, Mill will claim that what justifies his advocacy of different levels of moral thinking for different circumstances is that these levels, properly employed, will themselves bring about the greatest balance of pleasure over pain.

7. Moral Epistemology and the Proof of Utilitarianism

> We have now, then, an answer to the question, of what sort of proof
> the principle of utility is susceptible.
>
> (4.9)

Mill was an empiricist. He believed that all our knowledge and understanding are based on the evidence of the senses. He even extended his
empiricism into the territory of mathematics, in his important work *A
System of Logic* (1843). So it is no surprise to find him criticizing in the first
chapter of *Utilitarianism* views which suggest that we have access to moral
knowledge independently of the senses.

Mill dismisses out of hand the idea that there is a 'moral sense' which
enables us to discern what is right and wrong in each particular case. He is
more willing to take seriously the idea that we have a moral sense by which
we can grasp moral principles. These principles, according to the so-called
'intuitive school', are self-evident, and are seen as such once the terms in
which they are couched are understood. Mill, however, objects that the
intuitionists rarely develop any kind of system for their ethics, or attempt
to provide a first principle by means of which to resolve conflicts between
less fundamental principles.

Mill allies himself with the 'inductive' school, who claim that moral
questions are 'questions of observation and experience' (1.3). He would
therefore deny that merely setting out the act utilitarian principle clearly
will be enough to demonstrate its correctness. Nor will it be possible to
offer a deductive proof of the principle, of the kind available in, say, mathematics. In matters of practice, proofs must rest on some unprovable
bedrock: 'The art of music is good, for the reason, among others, that it
produces pleasure; but what proof is it possible to give that pleasure is
good?' (1.5). But that does not mean that morality is, in the end, merely a
matter of taste: 'Considerations may be presented capable of determining
the intellect either to give or withhold its assent to the doctrine; and this is
equivalent to proof' (1.5).

Mill's attempt to ground utilitarianism on observation and experience
constitutes the fourth chapter of utilitarianism. He begins that chapter by
referring back to the point made in chapter 1 that ultimate ends cannot be
deductively proven. He suggests that the same is true of 'matters of fact',
the first principles of our knowledge of the world. In the case of facts, one
can make an immediate appeal to the senses. I tell you it is raining, and you
ask for the evidence. I cannot prove it deductively, but I can take you to the

window and show you the rain falling. Mill wonders whether there is any faculty—of course it cannot be a moral sense—to which we might appeal in the case of practical ends, and goes on to suggest that there is: desire. His proof of utilitarianism consists in an appeal to the reader to reflect on their desires. It comes in three stages:

(1) happiness is desirable;
(2) the general happiness is desirable;
(3) nothing other than happiness is desirable.

There are difficulties with each stage, as we shall now see.

Stage 1: 'Visible' and 'Desirable'

The third paragraph of the fourth chapter of *Utilitarianism* is the most notorious in Mill's writings. It includes both stages 1 and 2 of the proof. Let us restrict ourselves for the present to stage 1. This first stage rests on an analogy between the notions of visibility and desirability, and came in for some stiff criticism from a later utilitarian, G. E. Moore: 'The fact is that "desirable" does not mean "able to be desired" as "visible" means "able to be seen". The desirable means simply what *ought* to be desired or deserves to be desired' (Moore 1903: 67).

Moore is quite right to point out this difference between visibility and desirability, but it is not necessary to read Mill's argument as resting on any analogy of the kind which Moore is criticizing. The analogy Mill is attempting to draw, admittedly in terms liable to confuse, is between matters of fact and ultimate ends of conduct. The idea is that, just as I can appeal to your visual sense in cases such as that of the rain outside, so I can appeal to your desire in the case of ultimate ends.

Mill is suggesting, then, that if you consider what you yourself desire, you will find that you desire pleasure, and that you desire it as an ultimate end. That, given that you have no reason to think of this desire as flawed or unacceptable in any way, should be sufficient to persuade you that pleasure is a good. By appealing to the fact of what his readers actually desire, and their observation of this fact, Mill believes that he has provided a sound 'inductive' argument for the claim that happiness or pleasure is desirable.

Stage 2: From the Happiness of Each to the Happiness of All

Mill concludes 4.3 with the claim that the fact that each person desires their own happiness is all the proof one could want 'that happiness is a good: that each person's happiness is a good to that person, and the general happiness, therefore, a good to the aggregate of persons'.

The problem here is that an egoist, who believes that the only reasons any person has to act are ultimately to pursue their own good, might accept the idea that they desire their own happiness. But, they might argue, it does not follow from this that the *overall* level of happiness should concern them in the slightest. What matters is how happy they themselves are.

Strictly, Mill's proof of utilitarianism is therefore unsuccessful. But it can be filled out with a number of assumptions, which the charitable reader may claim lie behind his argument in the text as it stands. First, we may assume, Mill is directing his argument primarily not to egoists, who have no concern for morality, but to those who, while accepting that there is a criterion of right and wrong, think of this criterion as non-utilitarian. So he will be assuming that his readers already believe that other people's happiness is of practical relevance. The question is in what way it is relevant.

Mill believes in a strong principle of impartiality. This principle emerges most clearly in a footnote to 5.36:

equal amounts of happiness are equally desirable, whether felt by the same or by different persons. This, however, is not a presupposition; not a premise needful to support the principle of utility, but the very principle itself . . . If there is any anterior principle implied, it can be no other than this, that the truths of arithmetic are applicable to the valuation of happiness, as of all other measurable quantities.

So Mill assumes both that happiness can be measured, and summed, and that when summing happiness the distinction between different people is irrelevant to action. The greater the happiness, the greater the good. He also believes that morality is *teleological*, in the sense that all moral rules must ultimately be based on the promotion of some good or end (*telos* is ancient Greek for 'end') (see for example 1.2).

These assumptions enable us to understand Mill's argument for utilitarianism in the following way. He sees his readers as already committed to the idea that the happiness of others must be given some weight in practical reasoning. Morality itself must be grounded on promotion of the good. If happiness is the only good (as stage 3 of the proof is meant to show), and it can and indeed should be aggregated and summed impartially, then we are led to act utilitarianism, the view that each person is morally required to maximize happiness overall.

There are, of course, problems with the assumptions that lie behind Mill's proof. First, the egoist will remain unpersuaded. Secondly, there are many questions about how happiness can be measured. Thirdly, the requirement that one be entirely impartial may appear unreasonable, in that it ignores the importance of the concern one has for oneself and one's friends and relatives. Finally, a non-consequentialist may argue that morality is not to be justified solely in terms of the good promoted; rather, it may be suggested, morality consists in certain categorical requirements which apply regardless of the good.

Stage 3: Nothing other than Happiness is Desirable

There remains one serious gap in Mill's proof, which he himself recognizes and indeed devotes most of chapter 4 to plugging. He has appealed to our desires to supply evidence for what is good or desirable. Plausibly enough, he suggests that we desire pleasure and that therefore we, who desire pleasure, should accept that pleasure is desirable. But do we not desire things other than pleasure? In particular, Mill's intuitionist opponents would have asked, do we not desire virtue?

One might have expected Mill at this point to draw a distinction between means and ends. Of course, he might say, we desire virtue, as we desire, say, food, or conversation, but only as a means to happiness. Happiness is the only thing that we desire as an end in itself. In fact, however, Mill allows that we do desire virtue 'as a thing desirable in itself' (4.5). He even admits that virtue is usually seen as something quite distinct from happiness, so it might appear that he is providing a counter-example to his thesis that happiness is the only end of all action.

In fact, however, Mill believes that the common view that happiness and virtue are separate is mistaken. Virtue, while not a means to happiness, is an ingredient of it, one of its 'parts'. What does Mill mean by this?

To understand his view we have first to return to Mill's associationism, according to which the aim of psychology and philosophy of mind is to describe the laws governing the succession of our mental states. Mill believes that mental states can be understood through their origins, and this is as true of desire as any other state. In the case of virtue, what happens is as follows. At first, one does indeed desire virtue as a means to happiness. But gradually one comes to associate virtue with happiness, and by degrees virtue comes to be desired for its own sake, 'either because the consciousness of it is a pleasure, or because the consciousness of being without it is a pain' (4.8). This view about the origin of desires for ends can be linked to the suggestion in 4.10 that 'to desire anything, except in proportion as the idea of it is pleasant, is a physical and metaphysical impossibility'. Mill's view, then, seems to be that the strength of any desire for an end is proportional to how pleasant the idea of that end is to the person who desires.

But associationism alone cannot explain how virtue is not desired as an end in itself independently of happiness. What Mill must be taken to mean is that, when we desire virtue, we desire the *enjoyable experience* of being virtuous or acting virtuously. Desire, he believes, just cannot 'be directed to anything ultimately except pleasure and exemption from pain' (4.11). My happiness, then, is not some 'collective something' (4.5), but is constituted by pleasurable experiences of various kinds—of music, virtue, and so on.

Mill's method of appealing to our desires appears to be the downfall of his proof. For, on reflection, many people find that they do in fact desire objects independently of pleasurable experience. Even in the case of food, it seems that one can distinguish the desire for the food from the desire for the pleasure consequent upon eating it. And in the case of desires for objects such as posthumous fame the distinction between object and pleasure is even clearer. If Mill is right in his claim that only pleasure is desired (and in his methodological assumptions), utilitarianism is proved. 'Whether it is so or not, must now be left to the considerations of the thoughtful reader' (4.12).

8. Moral Motivation

> The deeply-rooted conception which every individual even now has of himself as a social being, tends to make him feel it one of his natural wants that there should be harmony between his feelings and aims and those of his fellow creatures.
>
> (3.11)

Chapter 3 of *Utilitarianism*—'Of the Ultimate Sanction of the Principle of Utility'—has received markedly less attention than those immediately preceding and succeeding it. This is regrettable, since it contains much of interest to contemporary moral philosophers, especially those interested in moral motivation, and the relation of morality to the well-being of the moral agent.

The question Mill asks himself in this chapter is twofold. First, what in fact will or could motivate people to act in accordance with the utilitarian views he is advocating in *Utilitarianism*? And, secondly, why *should* anyone feel obligated so to act? Mill accepts that, unlike customary morality, utilitarianism does not come with its own sense of bindingness. Most, if not all, of us are already motivated to act in accordance with customary morality. But this is because of the way we have been brought up. Mill wants to suggest, then, that moral education should be directed at instilling in us a utilitarian motivation.

Such a moral education will involve using the so-called 'sanctions' of morality. The term 'sanction' has fallen out of use in recent moral philosophy. In the eighteenth and nineteenth centuries, it was used to refer to the sources of the pleasures and pains that in fact motivate people to act. Sanctions, then, fall into classes, one of which is constituted by the moral sanctions. Mill divides this class itself into two: internal and external. External sanctions depend on others directly, and include the hope of their favour and the fear of their anger. The internal sanction is the conscience or sense of duty of individuals themselves. It is engendered through education by others, but then takes on a life of its own. Mill suggests that both external and internal sanctions could be harnessed to utilitarianism.

So that is the answer to the first question, concerning *how* utilitarianism might motivate people. But it leaves the second question—why *should* we so arrange moral education?—unanswered. Mill's answer to this question is in the two moving paragraphs that close chapter 3. He suggests that there is a natural sentiment in human beings which encourages social life. Each person desires to be in harmony with others, and, Mill claims, this has the result that human beings will find their own individual greatest happiness in living in accordance with utilitarianism. Living in such a way will be one of the higher pleasures.

So here we have a second argument for utilitarianism, independent of the proof. Mill's proof rests on the notion that the utilitarian conception of impartiality itself grounds moral reasons for an agent. But he also believes that individuals who extend their sympathies in a utilitarian direction will live lives which are better for them in *self-interested* terms. This claim emerges directly from the ancient philosophers, especially Aristotle, by whom Mill was so influenced. It is a brave and exciting suggestion, implying that there is no reason for any individual to shy away from moral concern for others out of self-interest. But attempts to close the gap entirely between morality and self-interest have always seemed implausible. It is one thing to say that greater concern for others can enhance one's own life, but another to suggest that there is no point at which one's own interests come into conflict with those of others. There are two fundamental facts in ethics: (i) there are others like me with lives to live; but (ii) my life is independent of theirs. Ignoring the second fact can cause problems for utilitarianism, as we shall see in the following and final section.

9. The Separateness of Persons: Integrity and Justice

> I must again repeat, what the assailants of utilitarianism seldom have the justice to acknowledge, that the happiness which forms the utilitarian standard of what is right in conduct, is not the agent's own happiness, but that of all concerned. As between his own happiness and that of others, utilitarianism requires him to be as strictly impartial as a disinterested and benevolent spectator.
>
> (2.18; cf. 5.36)

According to act utilitarianism, I am required to perform that action which maximizes *overall* happiness, that is, the overall *amount* of happiness. In a sense, then, utilitarianism sees individual people and animals as mere 'receptacles' for happiness: the 'separateness' of persons is a morally neutral fact about the world. Where or when the happiness or unhappiness occurs, that is, *whose* happiness or unhappiness it is, is in itself of no importance. This has the result that utilitarianism faces objections from two directions: first, that of the personal concerns of the individual agent; secondly, that of moral principles concerning justice, rights, and equality, which rest on the importance of the distinctness of individuals.

The first strand of objection, that concerning the importance attached by the agent to their own personal concerns, can be found in the work of Bernard Williams, and in particular in his account of what has come to be known as 'the integrity objection'. There are, in fact, several lines of thought gathered under the heading of 'integrity', and I shall attempt here just to bring out a few of these.

Williams's argument begins with a pair of now famous examples.

GEORGE

George, a qualified chemist with wife and young children to support, is finding it hard to get a job. An older colleague tells George that he can get George a reasonably well-paid job in a laboratory where research is done on chemical and biological warfare. George turns down the job because of his opposition to such warfare. His colleague points out that the work is going to be done anyway, and that, were George not to take the post, the person appointed would probably be more zealous in advancing research than George.

JIM

Jim, a botanist travelling in South America, comes upon a public execution in a small town. A military captain has lined up twenty Indians. He explains to Jim that they have been chosen at random from the local population, which has recently been protesting against the government. The captain offers Jim a guest's privilege. If Jim wishes, he can select one of the Indians and shoot him; the other nineteen will then go free. Otherwise, the execution by the captain's henchman, Pedro, will go ahead as planned.

Williams claims that act utilitarianism is committed to the views not only that George should take the job and Jim shoot the Indian, but that it is *obvious* that they should do these things. This is true, however, only of 'single-level' versions of act utilitarianism. Multi-level versions, such as Mill's, might suggest that, outside the study, people should use customary moral principles to guide their action. The cases of George and Jim then become as murky and complex for the utilitarian as for anyone else.

A second aspect of the integrity objection concerns the notion of responsibility. Imagine that George does not take the job, and that Jim refuses to shoot. If George's zealous colleague develops some appalling weapons, which are then put to use, or if the captain orders Pedro to shoot the Indians, most of us would not ordinarily hold either George or Jim responsible for what has happened. Utilitarianism, however, puts both of them on the same level as the zealous colleague and the captain. This is utilitarianism's doctrine of *negative responsibility*, that I am as responsible for things I fail to prevent as I am for things I myself bring about.

Here utilitarianism does indeed face a problem. What the utilitarian should do is to point out how much weight Williams has to put on customary morality and its deliverances. The utilitarian account of responsibility is doubtless at odds here with customary morality, which holds people particularly responsible for what they do rather than what they fail to prevent (my not sending more money to development charities is not thought to be on a par with my sending poisoned food to the developing world, even though the outcome of each is the same). But, on reflection, this account of responsibility may itself seem hard to justify, especially in the light of a plausible account, such as Mill's in 5.13–14, of the origin of morality in legal restrictions with no independent justificatory weight of their own.

Nevertheless, there does seem to be something to the integrity objection, which emerges when one considers the importance of the fact that each agent carries out their moral deliberation from their own perspective, not from some imaginary 'God's eye view'. The relationships I have to others, and the importance to me of how well my own life goes, appear to ground reasons which are in conflict with the impartial act utilitarian principle. Consider the following two grisly variations of the Jim case.

JIM 2

Because the captain suspects him of involvement, Jim 2 is asked to commit suicide to save the Indians.

JIM 3

Jim 3 has lived in the area for some time, and has developed a deep personal relationship with one of the Indians. The captain, knowing of this, sadistically offers Jim 3 a choice: either he shoots the Indian and the other nineteen will go free, or the other nineteen will be shot and his friend will be freed.

In these cases, according to act utilitarianism, Jim 2 has no ultimate reason to give his interests special weight in his deliberations, and Jim 3 has no ultimate reason to take his special relationship into account. Both of these claims seem hard to accept: the separateness of persons does carry weight at the foundational level of practical deliberation.

It carries weight not just at the level of personal concern, but at that of morality itself, as we shall now see. This is the problem of justice, to which Mill devotes the longest chapter of *Utilitarianism*. Consider first another case.

THE SHERIFF

A town in the Wild West has been plagued by a series of violent crimes. The sheriff is confronted by a deputation led by the mayor. The deputation tells him that, unless he hangs the vagrant he has in his jail, whom the whole town believes to be the criminal, there will without doubt be a terrible riot, in which many people will almost certainly be killed or maimed. This vagrant has no friends or family. The sheriff knows he is innocent.

Mill's multi-level act utilitarianism would not advocate that sheriffs and others in their position consciously attempt to maximize happiness, for such attempts, it could plausibly be claimed, would probably tend to backfire, thus leading to less overall happiness in the long run. Nevertheless, imagine that in the case just described, for whatever reason, the sheriff does go ahead and hang the innocent vagrant. According to act utilitarianism, he has done the right thing. Is this not a terrible violation of human rights?

In chapter 5, Mill attempts to defuse the problem posed by justice for utilitarianism with an account of the origin of our sense of justice. Mill argues that all of morality has its origin in conformity to law. At first, laws were set down and the notion of legal obligation took root. This led to the emergence of a sense of obligation to obey those laws that it was felt *ought* to exist, and this sense of obligation is moral obligation. Mill distinguishes two kinds of obligation: perfect and imperfect. Both are, of course, genuine obligations, but in the case of imperfect obligations, such as that to be generous, the agent has some discretion in deciding when and in relation to whom to discharge the obligation. Perfect obligations, however, such as that not to murder another person, bind everyone all the time. These obligations correlate to certain rights. Thus, we might suggest, in the sheriff case, the vagrant had a right not to be murdered and the sheriff a perfect obligation not to murder him.

Mill argues that there are two elements in the idea of justice: a belief that someone has been harmed, and the desire to punish the person who causes that harm. The desire to punish itself has a dual origin, in the natural impulse to defend oneself, combined with the natural feeling of sympathy human beings have for one another. Our sense of justice, he goes on to argue, is aroused in response to serious attacks on central components of human well-being, in particular, the need for security. He concludes that utilitarianism itself will therefore support the sense of justice, since respecting that sense will in the long run maximize happiness.

It is not clear, however, that this multi-level response to the problem of justice is sufficient. Many people, even if they accept Mill's account of the origin of their sense of justice, will continue to believe that it provides insight into moral reasons which are not themselves subsumable under utilitarianism. In other words, they will believe that human beings *really* have rights, not just that it is useful from the utilitarian point of view for us to act as if this belief were true.

The same sort of difficulty emerges with equality and fairness. Imagine that you can bring about only one of the following outcomes:

Equality		Inequality	
Group 1	Group 2	Group 1	Group 2
50	50	90	20

Assume that each group contains, say, a thousand individuals. The numbers are meant roughly to represent happiness or welfare, so all those in *Equality* will have equally good lives, while those in *Inequality* will have lives either much better or much worse than the lives in *Equality*. The act utilitarian is committed to the view that *Inequality* is preferable, but this seems to ignore the fact that welfare is distributed equally between people in *Equality*. Fairness requires us to give some priority to those who would otherwise be worse off, and speaks in favour of choosing *Equality*. And, again, there is no compulsion to accept the view that our beliefs about fairness are any less plausible in themselves than any belief we might have in the utilitarian principle.

In this Section, I have tried to describe a set of interconnected problems which arise for act utilitarianism through its failure to put weight on the separateness of persons. The general utilitarian response to the kinds of case we have been discussing is to suggest that the moral beliefs that underpin our response themselves have utilitarian value. But the difficulty here, however, is in the claim that the utilitarian principle has epistemic priority.

It has to be admitted, however, that the opponents of utilitarianism have failed to show either that the utilitarian principle does not have this priority or that some other conflicting principle does. At present in moral philosophy, there is something of a stand-off between competing moral theories. What is required is further inquiry into moral justification and moral epistemology, and that will, I suggest, involve much deeper reflection than is common at present on the origin of our moral beliefs. There was a movement towards this in the latter half of the nineteenth century, in which Mill's chapter 5 played an important part, but it was unfortunately derailed by the confident intuitionism of G. E. Moore (1873–1958), W. D. Ross (1877–1971), and others. Despite the problems with Mill's account of the relation between utilitarianism and justice, his attempt to explain the peculiar phenomenon of morality was an important move in the right direction.

Further Reading

WHAT QUESTIONS IS MILL TRYING TO ANSWER?

Socrates' question can be found in Plato (c.385 BC/1979), *Gorgias*, trans. T. Irwin, Oxford: 500ᶜ3–4. The Platonic-Socratic view is more fully spelled out in Plato (c.380 BC/1992), *Republic*, trans. G. M. A. Grube, Indianapolis. Subjectivism in ethics is discussed in J. Rachels (1991), 'Subjectivism', in P. Singer (ed.), *A Companion to Ethics*, Oxford.

WHAT ARE THE ALTERNATIVES TO UTILITARIANISM?

Aristotle's views can be read in Aristotle (c.330 BC/1985), *Nicomachean Ethics*, trans. T. Irwin, Indianapolis. On modern virtue ethics, see the introduction and papers in R. Crisp and M. Slote (eds.) (1997), *Oxford Readings in Virtue Ethics*, Oxford. Kant's most well-known work in ethics is I. Kant (1785/1995), *Foundations of the Metaphysics of Morals*, trans. L. W. Beck, Upper Saddle River, NJ. His ethical works are usefully collected in I. Kant (1996), *Practical Philosophy*, trans. and ed. M. Gregor, Cambridge. For a discussion, see O. O'Neill (1991), 'Kantian Ethics', in P. Singer (ed.), *A Companion to Ethics*, Oxford.

JOHN STUART MILL AND UTILITARIANISM

Mill's *Autobiography* is one of the classics of English literature, and provides much insight into his understanding of himself and his views. The best biography is M. Packe (1954), *The Life of John Stuart Mill*, London. Mill's major ethical works are collected in volume 10 of the *Collected Works*, and repay serious study. The best accounts of Mill's philosophy as a whole are A. Ryan (1970), *The Philosophy of John Stuart Mill*, London; A. Ryan (1974), *J. S. Mill*, London; and J. Skorupski (1989), *John Stuart Mill*, London. An excellent book devoted to his ethics and political theory is F. Berger (1984), *Happiness, Justice, and Freedom*, Berkeley and Los Angeles. R. Crisp (1997), *Mill on Utilitarianism*, London, concentrates on Mill's *Utilitarianism*. For a general discussion of modern utilitarianism, see J. Griffin (1982), 'Modern Utilitarianism', *Revue Internationale de Philosophie*, 141.

HAPPINESS

Bentham's hedonism is outlined in J. Bentham (1789/1996), *Introduction to the Principles of Morals and Legislation*, ed. J. H. Burns and H. L. A. Hart, Oxford: chs.

1, 4–5. On theories of welfare in general, see D. Parfit (1984), *Reasons and Persons*, Oxford: app. 1, and J. Griffin (1986), *Well-Being*, Oxford: chs. 1–4. On the quantity/quality distinction, see R. Martin (1972), 'A Defence of Mill's Qualitative Hedonism', *Philosophy*, 47; H. R. West (1976), 'Mill's Qualitative Hedonism', *Philosophy*, 51; and L. W. Sumner (1992), 'Welfare, Happiness and Pleasure', *Utilitas*, 4. An early version of the alleged dilemma for Mill is to be found in T. H. Green (1883), *Prolegomena to Ethics*, Oxford: 167–78. The experience machine is discussed in R. Nozick (1974), *Anarchy, State, and Utopia*, Oxford: 42–5, and J. Glover (1984), *What Sort of People Should There Be?*, Harmondsworth: chs. 7–8.

FORMS OF UTILITARIANISM

Motive utilitarianism is most famously discussed in R. M. Adams (1976), 'Motive Utilitarianism', *Journal of Philosophy*, 73. The focus of utilitarianism is considered in R. Crisp (1992), 'Utilitarianism and the Life of Virtue', *Philosophical Quarterly*, 42. Contemporary debate concerning consequentialism is outlined well in S. Scheffler (ed.) (1988), *Consequentialism and its Critics*, Oxford: introduction. A seminal discussion of the forms of utilitarianism is that of D. Lyons (1965), *The Forms and Limits of Utilitarianism*, Oxford. The subjective/objective distinction is discussed in H. Sidgwick (1907), *The Methods of Ethics*, 7th edn., London: 207–10. There is a sophisticated discussion of total and average utilitarianism in D. Parfit (1984), *Reasons and Persons*, Oxford: pt. 4. A defence of rule utilitarianism can be found in B. Hooker (1995), 'Rule-Consequentialism, Incoherence, Fairness', *Proceedings of the Aristotelian Society*, 95, and a rule utilitarian interpretation of Mill is provided by J. O. Urmson (1953), 'The Interpretation of the Moral Philosophy of J. S. Mill', *Philosophical Quarterly*, 3.

LEVELS OF MORAL THINKING

The distinction between the criterion of morality and the decision procedures of moral agents is clearly made by R. E. Bales (1971), 'Act Utilitarianism: Account of Right-Making Characteristics or Decision-Making Procedure?', *American Philosophical Quarterly*, 8. A sophisticated recent discussion is that of P. Railton (1984), 'Alienation, Consequentialism, and the Demands of Morality', *Philosophy and Public Affairs*, 13. The most developed form of multi-level utilitarianism is to be found in R. M. Hare (1981), *Moral Thinking: Its Methods, Levels, and Point*, Oxford. The charge of incoherence against such a view is pressed by B. Williams (1985), *Ethics and the Limits of Philosophy*, London: ch. 6.

MORAL EPISTEMOLOGY AND THE PROOF OF UTILITARIANISM

An excellent early analysis and defence of Mill's proof is that of J. Seth (1908), 'The Alleged Fallacies in Mill's "Utilitarianism"', *Philosophical Review*, 17. The critique by G. E. Moore (1903), *Principia Ethica*, Cambridge: ch. 3, is essential reading. Other useful works include those of E. R. Hall (1949), 'The "Proof" of Utility in Bentham and Mill', *Ethics*, 60; A. N. Prior (1949), *Logic and the Basis of Ethics*, Oxford: ch. 1; D. P. Dryer (1969), 'Essay on Mill's *Utilitarianism*', introd. to J. S. Mill, *Collected Works*, ed. J. Robson, Toronto, vol. 10, and H. Putnam (1981), *Reason, Truth, and History*, Cambridge. A useful collection concerning moral epistemology is that of W. Sinnott-Armstrong and M. Timmons (eds.) (1996), *Moral Knowledge?*, New York.

MORAL MOTIVATION

On sanctions, it is best to read some of the works that influenced Mill, such as Plato (*c.*380 BC/1992), *Republic*, trans. G. M. A. Grube, Indianapolis: bks. 1–2, 4; Aristotle (*c.*330 BC/1985), *Nicomachean Ethics*, trans. T. Irwin, Indianapolis: bk. 1; J. Butler (1726/1897), *Works*, ed. W. E. Gladstone, Oxford: sermons 2–3; D. Hume (1751/1975), *An Enquiry concerning the Principles of Morals*, ed. L. Selby-Bigge, Oxford: sect. 9; A. Smith (1759/1976), *A Theory of the Moral Sentiments*, ed. D. D. Raphael and A. L. Macfie, Oxford: pt. 1, sect. 1; I. Kant (1785/1995), *Foundations of the Metaphysics of Morals*, trans, L. W. Beck, Upper Saddle River, NJ; and J. Bentham (1789/1996), *Introduction to the Principles of Morals and Legislation*, ed. J. H. Burns and H. L. A. Hart, Oxford: ch. 3.

THE SEPARATENESS OF PERSONS: INTEGRITY AND JUSTICE

The key statement of the integrity objection, including the cases of George and Jim, is to be found in B. Williams (1973), 'A Critique of Utilitarianism', in J. Smart and B. Williams, *Utilitarianism For and Against*, Cambridge: sects. 3–5. Good discussions can be found in J. Harris (1974), 'Williams on Negative Responsibility and Integrity', *Philosophical Quarterly*, 24; N. Davis (1980), 'Utilitarianism and Responsibility', *Ratio*, 22; and M. Hollis (1995), 'The Shape of a Life', in J. Altham and R. Harrison (eds.), *World, Mind, and Ethics*, Cambridge. The case of the sheriff is adapted from H. J. McCloskey (1957), 'An Examination of Restricted Utilitarianism', *Philosophical Review*, 66. Important in the interpretation of Mill on justice are D. Lyons (1994), *Rights, Welfare, and Mill's Moral Theory*, Oxford: essays 2, 3, 6; and F. Berger (1984), *Happiness, Justice, and Freedom*, Berkeley and Los Angeles: ch. 4. A good collection of writings on justice is to be found in A. Ryan (ed.) (1993), *Justice*, Oxford.

Analysis of *Utilitarianism*

Chapter 1. General Remarks

1–3. Fundamental Moral Disagreement
1. After more than two thousand years, the question of what is the ultimate moral principle remains controversial.
2. There is also disagreement concerning the ultimate principle in the sciences, but there the question is of less practical importance.
3. The idea of a natural moral faculty cannot help, nor can intuitionism.

4. The Tacit Influence of Utilitarianism
4. Because people have always been concerned about happiness, the utilitarian or greatest-happiness principle has had a major though unrecognized influence on moral beliefs. This is true of philosophies also, for example, that of Kant.

5–6. Plan of Text: Account, Defence, Proof
5. I shall offer both an account of utilitarianism and considerations in favour of it, equivalent to a proof. But note that an ordinary, direct proof of any end is not possible.
6. Before offering these considerations, I shall outline utilitarianism and deal with some objections to it.

Chapter 2. What Utilitarianism Is

1–2. Utility and Utilitarianism
1. 'Utility' is not 'the useful', as opposed to 'pleasure' or 'the pleasurable'. Utility *is* pleasure, so utilitarianism cannot be criticized (or indeed praised) for its antipathy to pleasures.
2. Utilitarianism: the right action is that which produces the greatest balance of happiness (pleasure) over unhappiness (pain). Pleasure and pain are the only goods (hedonism).

3–9. The Philosophy of Swine Objection and Response (Higher Pleasures)
3. Some claim that hedonistic utilitarianism, since it suggests that nothing is good except pleasure, is a philosophy worthy of pigs.
4. But hedonists can respond that humans, because of their higher faculties, are capable of pleasures beyond those of pigs. These include the pleasures of the intellect and of moral and other sentiments. Utilitarians can suggest that these pleasures are more valuable both because of their being more permanent and so on, and because of their quality.

5. A higher pleasure is one preferred to any amount of a lower pleasure by someone who has experienced both.

6. Those who have experienced both do prefer the pleasures involved in exercising their higher faculties. This can be put down to the human sense of dignity. Contentment is to be distinguished from happiness.

7. Objection: some people who have experienced both sometimes go for lower pleasure. Answer: this is consistent with their knowing they are choosing the less valuable pleasure. Objection: some people lose their enthusiasm for the higher pleasures. Answer: they do not choose this, having become incapable of higher pleasure.

8. The quantity of a pleasure, and the relative value of a pleasure as against a pain, can also only be decided by asking those who have experienced them.

9. Utilitarians will advocate nobleness of character anyway, because of its beneficial consequences for people other than the agent.

10. *Summary*

    10. The Greatest Happiness Principle: the ultimate end is the greatest balance of pleasure over pain, to be assessed by competent judges. This being the end of human action, it is also the end of morality, which consists of those rules that will best further the end.

11. *The Unattainability and Renunciation Objections*

    11. 'Happiness is unattainable. Happiness can be renounced and doing so is necessary for virtue.'

12. *Response to the Unattainability Objection*

    12. Even if happiness is unattainable, acting to decrease suffering would be worthwhile. Continual pleasurable excitement is impossible, but a broader kind of happiness is possible.

13–14. *The Non-satisfaction Objection and Response*

    13. 'Human beings would not be satisfied with a moderate share of such happiness.' But many have been satisfied with less. This conception of happiness includes both tranquillity and excitement. Selfishness and lack of cultivation are the main causes of unhappiness.

    14. Cultivation could be widespread in civilized countries, nor need people be selfish. If human affairs continue to improve, the evils of the world will be greatly reduced.

15–18. *Response to the Renunciation Objection*

    15. Happiness can indeed be renounced, as by heroes. But this is admirable only when done for the sake of the happiness of others.

    16. It is worth adding that, in the world as it is, the readiness to do without happiness is the best way to achieve it.

    17. Utilitarians admire only self-sacrifice for the sake of the happiness of others.

    18. The agent is required by utilitarianism to be impartial between his own

happiness and that of others. To approach the utilitarian ideal, laws should seek to make the pursuit of individual happiness as close as possible to pursuit of overall happiness, and education and opinion should establish an association between the two in the mind of each agent.

19. *The Demandingness Objection and Response*

19. 'The utilitarian demand that one always act to promote the good of all is excessive.' But this confuses the standard of morals with the motive for action. Utilitarians claim that motives are morally irrelevant. In the case of actions from duty, utilitarianism usually requires that the agent concerns herself not with the good of humanity as a whole, but with a small subset. The agent will, however, refrain from certain actions because of their consequences for society as a whole.

20–21. *The Coldness Objection and Response*

20. 'Utilitarianism, because of its emphasis on calculation, chills the moral sentiments people feel towards one another.' Utilitarians, like all moral theorists, do judge actions independently of the qualities of the agent. Nor do utilitarians think that only virtue matters. No do they rigidly calculate that a right action is always indicative of virtue or a wrong one always indicative of vice. But there are strong connections between virtue and right action.

21. If the objection is that some utilitarians fail to pay sufficient attention to qualities of character, it can be accepted; but even they err on the right side.

22. *The Godless Objection and Response*

22. Whether utilitarianism is godless depends on our conception of God. If he is benevolent, then this is consistent with the utilitarian emphasis on happiness. If his revealed will is meant to be the foundation of morals, utilitarians can claim that such revelations are utilitarian. Another view is that ethics is required to interpret the will of God.

23. *The Expediency Objection and Response*

23. 'Utilitarianism is concerned with expediency, not principle.' Expediency can be taken to concern self-interest, or what is immediately beneficial, but involves the violation of some more useful rule. Utilitarianism is not based on either, though it will allow that in some special circumstances rules can be broken.

24. *The Shortage-of-Time Objection and Response*

24. 'There is insufficient time to calculate the effects of actions on the general happiness.' Mankind has been learning the tendencies of actions for a long time. Utilitarianism allows for the use of secondary principles.

25. *The Temptation Objection and Response*

25. 'Utilitarians will make exceptions to moral rules.' But any moral theory supplies people with the material for excuses. And the utilitarian principle

at least makes possible the resolution of practical conflicts between competing considerations.

Chapter 3. Of the Ultimate Sanction of the Principle of Utility

1–2. Sanctions and Moral Standards
1. It is often asked of moral standards that depart from customary morality, which already rests on a feeling of obligation, what their sanction is, that is, where their alleged binding force emerges from.
2. Such a question will continue to be asked of utilitarianism until moral education improves.

3. External Sanctions
3. Utilitarianism can be supported by the social and religious sanctions.

4–5. The Internal Sanction
4. The nature of conscience.
5. Utilitarianism can be supported by conscience.

6–8. The Origin of the Internal Sanction
6. Some say that those who believe moral obligation to be subjective will be less morally motivated. But, if so, this will not be a special problem for utilitarianism, and objectivists can also ignore their consciences.
7. The objectivist intuitionist view of the innate moral sense is anyway not inconsistent with utilitarianism.
8. Furthermore, if the sense of obligation is acquired, it is natural and can be attached to utilitarianism.

9–11. The Natural Basis of Sentiment
9. The sense of obligation, created artificially, can be weakened through reflection.
10. Utilitarianism, however, would be secure, as it is grounded in the natural social feelings of humanity.
11. Some people already feel moral obligation sufficiently for them to act on utilitarianism.

Chapter 4. Of What Sort of Proof the Principle of Utility is Susceptible

1–3. Proof that Happiness is one of the Criteria of Morality
1. Ultimate ends cannot be proved by reasoning. But matters of fact can be tested by the senses. Is there anything analogous to such a test in the case of ends?
2. An end is something that is desirable. The utilitarian view is that happiness

is the only thing desirable. What is required for this doctrine to be accepted?

3. Visibility is tested by sight; desirability is tested by desire. The fact that each person desires his own happiness is sufficient proof that the general happiness is desirable.

4–12. *Proof that Happiness Alone is Desired*

4. Problem: people seem to desire things other than happiness, such as virtue.

5. Utilitarianism accepts that virtue is desired for its own sake, but as part of happiness.

6. The same can be said of, for example, money.

7. According to utilitarianism, the cultivation of virtue is more important than anything for the general happiness.

8. Therefore nothing is desired except happiness. People desire virtue either because the consciousness of it is pleasurable, or because consciousness of its absence is painful.

9. Therefore if human beings do desire nothing other than happiness, utilitarianism will be proven.

10. Introspection will demonstrate that thinking of a thing as desirable and thinking of it as pleasant are the same.

11. One can will virtuous actions independently of thinking them pleasurable. But this is not a problem for the proof, since what arises from habit has no claim to being good. Habitual virtue is merely a means to what is good in itself.

12. If the doctrine that pleasure alone is good is true, utilitarianism is proven. The reader must now decide whether it is true.

Chapter 5. On the Connexion between Justice and Utility

1–2. *The Problem of Justice*

1. Belief in a principle of justice, opposed to utilitarianism, is often seen as natural.

2. Because a belief is natural does not mean that we have to act upon it nor that it is a response to an objective reality. We must ask whether our sentiments of justice stand on their own, or whether they might not be themselves explained in utilitarian terms.

3–10. *The Spheres of Justice*

3. First we must decide whether there is anything common to the conduct described as unjust. If there is, we must then see whether we can explain how the sentiment of justice might have arisen.

4. Which things are called unjust?

5. First sphere: legal rights. It is thought unjust to deprive someone of what they possess by legal right.
6. Second sphere: moral rights. Some laws are themselves thought to be unjust, and so to violate people's moral rights.
7. Third sphere: desert. It is thought unjust if someone receives a good or bad he does not deserve.
8. Fourth sphere: contracts. It is thought unjust to break engagements with others voluntarily entered into.
9. Fifth sphere: impartiality. It is thought unjust to be inappropriately partial.
10. Sixth sphere: equality. Each person thinks that justice requires equality, except when inequality is more beneficial overall.

11–12. *The Etymology of Justice: Its Origin in Law*
11. What is the mental link between all these usages of the term 'justice'? Let us consider its history through its etymology.
12. The origin of 'justice' is in the idea of conformity to actual law. It then came to be used to refer to violations of ideal laws.

13–15. *Justice, Punishment, and Moral Obligation*
13. Even in spheres where law is inappropriate, the idea of ideal law remains: we think that injustice deserves punishment, by public disapproval if not by law.
14. Penal sanction, however, is at the heart of moral obligation in general, as opposed to simple expediency.
15. Justice is to be characterized in terms of rights.

16–23. *The Origin of the Sentiment of Justice*
16. Where did the feeling which accompanies this idea of justice come from? Could it have come out of a concern for the general happiness?
17. No, but what is moral in it does.
18. The two elements of the sentiment of justice are (i) the desire to punish someone who has done harm and (ii) the belief that some definite individual has been harmed.
19. The desire to punish emerges from (i) the impulse of self-defence and (ii) the feeling of sympathy.
20. Animals naturally defend themselves and their young. Human sympathy is broader, extending to all sentient beings, and more intelligent. The human impulse is excited by any perceived threat to society as a whole.
21. What is moral in the sentiment of justice arises from its being felt only at threats to the general good, as opposed to mere self-interest.
22. Objection: the sentiment of justice sometimes concerns itself not with harm to society, but only with that to certain individuals. Response: the just person will be aware that the rule he asserts is for the benefit of others.
23. Summary of argument so far.

24–5. *Rights and Utility*

24. A right to something is having a valid claim on society to protect one's possession of that thing.

25. The only reason society ought to offer its protection is general utility. The sentiment of justice is felt so strongly because of the importance for our well-being of what it is concerned with: security.

26–31. *The Ambiguity of Justice*

26. If justice is a self-evident standard independent of utility, why is there so much disagreement about it?

27. Individuals themselves hold conflicting principles of justice.

28. For example, there are several views on the justice of punishment: (i) punishment is just only when in the interest of the offender; (ii) punishment is just only when carried out for deterrence; (iii) no action is free, so no punishment is just.

29. And on how punishments are to fit crimes: (i) the eye for an eye view; (ii) punishment should be proportionate to guilt; (iii) punishment should be proportionate to the need for deterrence.

30. And on how labour is to be rewarded: (i) talent or skill should be rewarded; (ii) they should not, since their possession is arbitrary.

31. And on taxation: (i) tax should be numerically proportional to means; (ii) tax should be progressive; (iii) (a view held only tacitly) each should pay the same.

32–3. *Rights and Utility: Reprise*

32. The rules of justice concern the most important conditions for well-being and therefore are of more stringent obligation. This is captured in the notion of rights.

33. These moral rules determine the social feelings of humanity, since they preserve peace, and each person has the strongest reason for encouraging others to obey them. The most obvious injustices are aggression or domination; then comes withholding what is due. Both involve the infliction of harm.

34–5. *The Importance of Desert*

34. The desire for vengeance leads to the return of evil for evil's being at the heart of justice. Failing to return good for good is also harmful.

35. Most maxims of justice are merely instrumental to returning evil for evil and good for good.

36. *Impartiality and Equality*

36. Impartiality and equality are necessary for carrying out the other obligations of justice, and can be seen as corollaries of those obligations. They also rest directly on the greatest happiness principle itself. (Note on Spencer: the assumption behind utilitarianism, and the nature of scientific

proof in ethics.) The principle of equality is constrained by the principle of utility.

37–8. *Conclusion*

37. The maxims of justice are extremely important, but can be overridden.

38. Summary of argument. Conclusion: justice is not a problem for utilitarianism.

The Text Printed in this Edition

Utilitarianism was first published in 1861 as a series of three essays in volume 64 of *Fraser's Magazine* (October: chs. 1 and 2, November: chs. 3 and 4, December: ch. 5). It was first published as a book in 1863. The second edition was published in 1864, and the third in 1867. The text used in the present edition is the fourth, of 1871, the last published in Mill's lifetime (in London, by Longmans, Green, Reader, and Dyer). I constructed the text by correcting the World's Classics edition (Oxford, 1991) against the original. The only deliberate changes I have made from the fourth edition are the addition of paragraph and line numbering, and the substitution of arabic for roman numbering of chapters. The fourth edition is also that used in the Toronto edition of the *Collected Works*. The notes below mention the more significant textual variations between the fourth and earlier editions.

PART 2
The Text

UTILITARIANISM

I

GENERAL REMARKS.

THERE are few circumstances among those which make up the present 1
condition of human knowledge, more unlike what might have been
expected, or more significant of the backward state in which speculation
on the most important subjects still lingers, than the little progress which
has been made in the decision of the controversy respecting the criterion 5
of right and wrong. From the dawn of philosophy, the question concerning the *summum bonum*, or, what is the same thing, concerning the foundation of morality, has been accounted the main problem in speculative
thought, has occupied the most gifted intellects, and divided them into
sects and schools, carrying on a vigorous warfare against one another. And 10
after more than two thousand years the same discussions continue,
philosophers are still ranged under the same contending banners, and
neither thinkers nor mankind at large seem nearer to being unanimous on
the subject, than when the youth Socrates listened to the old Protagoras,
and asserted (if Plato's dialogue be grounded on a real conversation) the 15
theory of utilitarianism against the popular morality of the so-called
sophist.

It is true that similar confusion and uncertainty, and in some cases 2
similar discordance, exist respecting the first principles of all the sciences,
not excepting that which is deemed the most certain of them, mathematics; without much impairing, generally indeed without impairing at all,
the trustworthiness of the conclusions of those sciences. An apparent 5
anomaly, the explanation of which is, that the detailed doctrines of a
science are not usually deduced from, nor depend for their evidence upon,
what are called its first principles. Were it not so, there would be no science
more precarious, or whose conclusions were more insufficiently made
out, than algebra; which derives none of its certainty from what are com- 10
monly taught to learners as its elements, since these, as laid down by some
of its most eminent teachers, are as full of fictions as English law, and of
mysteries as theology. The truths which are ultimately accepted as the first

principles of a science, are really the last results of metaphysical analysis,
15 practised on the elementary notions with which the science is conversant;
and their relation to the science is not that of foundations to an edifice, but
of roots to a tree, which may perform their office equally well though they
be never dug down to and exposed to light. But though in science the particular truths precede the general theory, the contrary might be expected
20 to be the case with a practical art, such as morals or legislation. All action is
for the sake of some end, and rules of action, it seems natural to suppose,
must take their whole character and colour from the end to which they are
subservient. When we engage in a pursuit, a clear and precise conception
of what we are pursuing would seem to be the first thing we need, instead
25 of the last we are to look forward to. A test of right and wrong must be the
means, one would think, of ascertaining what is right or wrong, and not a
consequence of having already ascertained it.

3   The difficulty is not avoided by having recourse to the popular theory of
a natural faculty, a sense or instinct, informing us of right and wrong.
For—besides that the existence of such a moral instinct is itself one of the
matters in dispute—those believers in it who have any pretensions to phil-
5 osophy, have been obliged to abandon the idea that it discerns what is right
or wrong in the particular case in hand, as our other senses discern the
sight or sound actually present. Our moral faculty, according to all those of
its interpreters who are entitled to the name of thinkers, supplies us only
with the general principles of moral judgments; it is a branch of our
10 reason, not of our sensitive faculty; and must be looked to for the abstract
doctrines of morality, not for perception of it in the concrete. The intuitive, no less than what may be termed the inductive, school of ethics,
insists on the necessity of general laws. They both agree that the morality
of an individual action is not a question of direct perception, but of the
15 application of a law to an individual case. They recognise also, to a great
extent, the same moral laws; but differ as to their evidence, and the source
from which they derive their authority. According to the one opinion, the
principles of morals are evident *à priori*, requiring nothing to command
assent, except that the meaning of the terms be understood. According to
20 the other doctrine, right and wrong, as well as truth and falsehood, are
questions of observation and experience. But both hold equally that
morality must be deduced from principles; and the intuitive school affirm
as strongly as the inductive, that there is a science of morals. Yet they
seldom attempt to make out a list of the *à priori* principles which are to
25 serve as the premises of the science; still more rarely do they make any

effort to reduce those various principles to one first principle, or common ground of obligation. They either assume the ordinary precepts of morals as of *à priori* authority, or they lay down as the common groundwork of those maxims, some generality much less obviously authoritative than the maxims themselves, and which has never succeeded in gaining popular   30 acceptance. Yet to support their pretensions there ought either to be some one fundamental principle or law, at the root of all morality, or if there be several, there should be a determinate order of precedence among them; and the one principle, or the rule of deciding between the various principles when they conflict, ought to be self-evident.   35

To inquire how far the bad effects of this deficiency have been mitigated   4 in practice, or to what extent the moral beliefs of mankind have been vitiated or made uncertain by the absence of any distinct recognition of an ultimate standard, would imply a complete survey and criticism of past and present ethical doctrine. It would, however, be easy to show that what-   5 ever steadiness or consistency these moral beliefs have attained, has been mainly due to the tacit influence of a standard not recognised. Although the non-existence of an acknowledged first principle has made ethics not so much a guide as a consecration of men's actual sentiments, still, as men's sentiments, both of favour and of aversion, are greatly influenced   10 by what they suppose to be the effects of things upon their happiness, the principle of utility, or as Bentham latterly called it, the greatest happiness principle, has had a large share in forming the moral doctrines even of those who most scornfully reject its authority. Nor is there any school of thought which refuses to admit that the influence of actions on happiness   15 is a most material and even predominant consideration in many of the details of morals, however unwilling to acknowledge it as the fundamental principle of morality, and the source of moral obligation. I might go much further, and say that to all those *à priori* moralists who deem it necessary to argue at all, utilitarian arguments are indispensable. It is not my present   20 purpose to criticize these thinkers; but I cannot help referring, for illustration, to a systematic treatise by one of the most illustrious of them, the *Metaphysics of Ethics*, by Kant. This remarkable man, whose system of thought will long remain one of the landmarks in the history of philosophical speculation, does, in the treatise in question, lay down an univer-   25 sal first principle as the origin and ground of moral obligation; it is this:—'So act, that the rule on which thou actest would admit of being adopted as a law by all rational beings.' But when he begins to deduce from this precept any of the actual duties of morality, he fails, almost

30 grotesquely, to show that there would be any contradiction, any logical (not to say physical) impossibility, in the adoption by all rational beings of the most outrageously immoral rules of conduct. All he shows is that the *consequences* of their universal adoption would be such as no one would choose to incur.

5   On the present occasion, I shall, without further discussion of the other theories, attempt to contribute something towards the understanding and appreciation of the Utilitarian or Happiness theory, and towards such proof as it is susceptible of. It is evident that this cannot be proof in the
5 ordinary and popular meaning of the term. Questions of ultimate ends are not amenable to direct proof. Whatever can be proved to be good, must be so by being shown to be a means to something admitted to be good without proof. The medical art is proved to be good, by its conducing to health; but how is it possible to prove that health is good? The art of music
10 is good, for the reason, among others, that it produces pleasure; but what proof is it possible to give that pleasure is good? If, then, it is asserted that there is a comprehensive formula, including all things which are in them-selves good, and that what ever else is good, is not so as an end, but as a mean, the formula may be accepted or rejected, but is not a subject of
15 what is commonly understood by proof. We are not, however, to infer that its acceptance or rejection must depend on blind impulse, or arbitrary choice. There is a larger meaning of the word proof, in which this question is as amenable to it as any other of the disputed questions of philosophy. The subject is within the cognizance of the rational faculty; and neither
20 does that faculty deal with it solely in the way of intuition. Considerations may be presented capable of determining the intellect either to give or withhold its assent to the doctrine; and this is equivalent to proof.

6   We shall examine presently of what nature are these considerations; in what manner they apply to the case, and what rational grounds, therefore, can be given for accepting or rejecting the utilitarian formula. But it is a preliminary condition of rational acceptance or rejection, that the formula
5 should be correctly understood. I believe that the very imperfect notion ordinarily formed of its meaning, is the chief obstacle which impedes its reception; and that could it be cleared, even from only the grosser miscon-ceptions, the question would be greatly simplified, and a large proportion of its difficulties removed. Before, therefore, I attempt to enter into the
10 philosophical grounds which can be given for assenting to the utilitarian standard, I shall offer some illustrations of the doctrine itself; with the view of showing more clearly what it is, distinguishing it from what it is not, and disposing of such of the practical objections to it as either origi-

nate in, or are closely connected with, mistaken interpretations of its meaning. Having thus prepared the ground, I shall afterwards endeavour to throw such light as I can upon the question, considered as one of philo-sophical theory. 15

2

WHAT UTILITARIANISM IS.

1   A PASSING remark is all that needs be given to the ignorant blunder of
supposing that those who stand up for utility as the test of right and
wrong, use the term in that restricted and merely colloquial sense in which
utility is opposed to pleasure. An apology is due to the philosophical oppo-
5   nents of utilitarianism, for even the momentary appearance of confound-
ing them with anyone capable of so absurd a misconception; which is
the more extraordinary, inasmuch as the contrary accusation, of referring
everything to pleasure, and that too in its grossest form, is another of
the common charges against utilitarianism: and, as has been pointedly
10 remarked by an able writer, the same sort of persons, and often the very
same persons, denounce the theory 'as impracticably dry when the word
utility precedes the word pleasure, and as too practicably voluptuous
when the word pleasure precedes the word utility.' Those who know anything about the matter are aware that every writer, from Epicurus to
15 Bentham, who maintained the theory of utility, meant by it, not something to be contradistinguished from pleasure, but pleasure itself, together
with exemption from pain; and instead of opposing the useful to the
agreeable or the ornamental, have always declared that the useful means
these, among other things. Yet the common herd, including the herd of
20 writers, not only in newspapers and periodicals, but in books of weight
and pretension, are perpetually falling into this shallow mistake. Having
caught up the word utilitarian, while knowing nothing whatever about it
but its sound, they habitually express by it the rejection, or the neglect, of
pleasure in some of its forms; of beauty, of ornament, or of amusement.
25 Nor is the term thus ignorantly misapplied solely in disparagement, but
occasionally in compliment; as though it implied superiority to frivolity
and the mere pleasures of the moment. And this perverted use is the only
one in which the word is popularly known, and the one from which the
new generation are acquiring their sole notion of its meaning. Those who
30 introduced the word, but who had for many years discontinued it as a dis-

tinctive appellation, may well feel themselves called upon to resume it, if by doing so they can hope to contribute anything towards rescuing it from this utter degradation.*

The creed which accepts as the foundation of morals, Utility, or the **2** Greatest Happiness Principle, holds that actions are right in proportion as they tend to promote happiness, wrong as they tend to produce the reverse of happiness. By happiness is intended pleasure, and the absence of pain; by unhappiness, pain, and the privation of pleasure. To give a clear 5 view of the moral standard set up by the theory, much more requires to be said; in particular, what things it includes in the ideas of pain and pleasure; and to what extent this is left an open question. But these supplementary explanations do not affect the theory of life on which this theory of morality is grounded—namely, that pleasure, and freedom from pain, are the 10 only things desirable as ends; and that all desirable things (which are as numerous in the utilitarian as in any other scheme) are desirable either for the pleasure inherent in themselves, or as means to the promotion of pleasure and the prevention of pain.

Now, such a theory of life excites in many minds, and among them in **3** some of the most estimable in feeling and purpose, inveterate dislike. To suppose that life has (as they express it) no higher end than pleasure—no better and nobler object of desire and pursuit—they designate as utterly mean and grovelling; as a doctrine worthy only of swine, to whom the 5 followers of Epicurus were, at a very early period, contemptuously likened; and modern holders of the doctrine are occasionally made the subject of equally polite comparisons by its German, French and English assailants.

When thus attacked, the Epicureans have always answered, that it is not **4** they, but their accusers, who represent human nature in a degrading light; since the accusation supposes human beings to be capable of no pleasures except those of which swine are capable. If this supposition were true, the charge could not be gainsaid, but would then be no longer an imputation; 5 for if the sources of pleasure were precisely the same to human beings and to swine, the rule of life which is good enough for the one would be good

---

* The author of this essay has reason for believing himself to be the first person who brought the word utilitarian into use. He did not invent it, but adopted it from a passing expression in Mr Galt's *Annals of the Parish*. After using it as a designation for several years, he and others abandoned it from a growing dislike to anything resembling a badge or watchword of sectarian distinction. But as a name for one single opinion, not a set of opinions—to denote the recognition of utility as a standard, not any particular way of applying it—the term supplies a want in the language, and offers, in many cases, a convenient mode of avoiding tiresome circumlocution.

enough for the other. The comparison of the Epicurean life to that of beasts is felt as degrading, precisely because a beast's pleasures do not satisfy a human being's conceptions of happiness. Human beings have faculties more elevated than the animal appetites, and when once made conscious of them, do not regard anything as happiness which does not include their gratification. I do not, indeed, consider the Epicureans to have been by any means faultless in drawing out their scheme of consequences from the utilitarian principle. To do this in any sufficient manner, many Stoic, as well as Christian elements require to be included. But there is no known Epicurean theory of life which does not assign to the pleasures of the intellect, of the feelings and imagination, and of the moral sentiments, a much higher value as pleasures than to those of mere sensation. It must be admitted, however, that utilitarian writers in general have placed the superiority of mental over bodily pleasures chiefly in the greater permanency, safety, uncostliness, &c., of the former—that is, in their circumstantial advantages rather than in their intrinsic nature. And on all these points utilitarians have fully proved their case; but they might have taken the other, and, as it may be called, higher ground, with entire consistency. It is quite compatible with the principle of utility to recognise the fact, that some *kinds* of pleasure are more desirable and more valuable than others. It would be absurd that while, in estimating all other things, quality is considered as well as quantity, the estimation of pleasures should be supposed to depend on quantity alone.

5   If I am asked, what I mean by difference of quality in pleasures, or what makes one pleasure more valuable than another, merely as a pleasure, except its being greater in amount, there is but one possible answer. Of two pleasures, if there be one to which all or almost all who have experience of both give a decided preference, irrespective of any feeling of moral obligation to prefer it, that is the more desirable pleasure. If one of the two is, by those who are competently acquainted with both, placed so far above the other that they prefer it, even though knowing it to be attended with a greater amount of discontent, and would not resign it for any quantity of the other pleasure which their nature is capable of, we are justified in ascribing to the preferred enjoyment a superiority in quality, so far outweighing quantity as to render it, in comparison, of small account.

6   Now it is an unquestionable fact that those who are equally acquainted with, and equally capable of appreciating and enjoying, both, do give a most marked preference to the manner of existence which employs their higher faculties. Few human creatures would consent to be changed into

any of the lower animals, for a promise of the fullest allowance of a beast's ₅
pleasures; no intelligent human being would consent to be a fool, no
instructed person would be an ignoramus, no person of feeling and conscience would be selfish and base, even though they should be persuaded
that the fool, the dunce, or the rascal is better satisfied with his lot than
they are with theirs. They would not resign what they possess more than ₁₀
he, for the most complete satisfaction of all the desires which they have in
common with him. If they ever fancy they would, it is only in cases of
unhappiness so extreme, that to escape from it they would exchange their
lot for almost any other, however undesirable in their own eyes. A being of
higher faculties requires more to make him happy, is capable probably of ₁₅
more acute suffering, and is certainly accessible to it at more points, than
one of an inferior type; but in spite of these liabilities, he can never really
wish to sink into what he feels to be a lower grade of existence. We may
give what explanation we please of this unwillingness; we may attribute it
to pride, a name which is given indiscriminately to some of the most and ₂₀
to some of the least estimable feelings of which mankind are capable; we
may refer it to the love of liberty and personal independence, an appeal to
which was with the Stoics one of the most effective means for the inculcation of it; to the love of power, or to the love of excitement, both of which
do really enter into and contribute to it: but its most appropriate appella- ₂₅
tion is a sense of dignity, which all human beings possess in one form or
other, and in some, though by no means in exact, proportion to their
higher faculties, and which is so essential a part of the happiness of those
in whom it is strong, that nothing which conflicts with it could be, otherwise than momentarily, an object of desire to them. Whoever supposes ₃₀
that this preference takes place at a sacrifice of happiness—that the superior being, in anything like equal circumstances, is not happier than the
inferior—confounds the two very different ideas, of happiness, and
content. It is indisputable that the being whose capacities of enjoyment
are low, has the greatest chance of having them fully satisfied; and a highly ₃₅
endowed being will always feel that any happiness which he can look for,
as the world is constituted, is imperfect. But he can learn to bear its imperfections, if they are at all bearable; and they will not make him envy the
being who is indeed unconscious of the imperfections, but only because
he feels not at all the good which those imperfections qualify. It is better to ₄₀
be a human being dissatisfied than a pig satisfied; better to be Socrates dissatisfied than a fool satisfied. And if the fool, or the pig, is of a different
opinion, it is because they only know their own side of the question. The
other party to the comparison knows both sides.

7   It may be objected, that many who are capable of the higher pleasures, occasionally, under the influence of temptation, postpone them to the lower. But this is quite compatible with a full appreciation of the intrinsic superiority of the higher. Men often, from infirmity of character, make
5 their election for the nearer good, though they know it to be the less valuable; and this no less when the choice is between two bodily pleasures, than when it is between bodily and mental. They pursue sensual indulgences to the injury of health, though perfectly aware that health is the greater good. It may be further objected, that many who begin with
10 youthful enthusiasm for everything noble, as they advance in years sink into indolence and selfishness. But I do not believe that those who undergo this very common change, voluntarily choose the lower description of pleasures in preference to the higher. I believe that before they devote themselves exclusively to the one, they have already become incapable of
15 the other. Capacity for the nobler feelings is in most natures a very tender plant, easily killed, not only by hostile influences, but by mere want of sustenance; and in the majority of young persons it speedily dies away if the occupations to which their position in life has devoted them, and the society into which it has thrown them, are not favourable to keeping that
20 higher capacity in exercise. Men lose their high aspirations as they lose their intellectual tastes, because they have not time or opportunity for indulging them; and they addict themselves to inferior pleasures, not because they deliberately prefer them, but because they are either the only ones to which they have access, or the only ones which they are any longer
25 capable of enjoying. It may be questioned whether any one who has remained equally susceptible to both classes of pleasures, ever knowingly and calmly preferred the lower; though many, in all ages, have broken down in an ineffectual attempt to combine both.

8   From this verdict of the only competent judges, I apprehend there can be no appeal. On a question which is the best worth having of two pleasures, or which of two modes of existence is the most grateful to the feelings, apart from its moral attributes and from its consequences, the
5 judgment of those who are qualified by knowledge of both, or, if they differ, that of the majority among them, must be admitted as final. And there needs be the less hesitation to accept this judgment respecting the quality of pleasures, since there is no other tribunal to be referred to even on the question of quantity. What means are there of determining which
10 is the acutest of two pains, or the intensest of two pleasurable sensations, except the general suffrage of those who are familiar with both? Neither pains nor pleasures are homogeneous, and pain is always heterogeneous

with pleasure. What is there to decide whether a particular pleasure is worth purchasing at the cost of a particular pain, except the feelings and judgment of the experienced? When, therefore, those feelings and judg- 15 ment declare the pleasures derived from the higher faculties to be prefer- able *in kind*, apart from the question of intensity, to those of which the animal nature, disjoined from the higher faculties, is susceptible, they are entitled on this subject to the same regard.

I have dwelt on this point, as being a necessary part of a perfectly just 9 conception of Utility or Happiness, considered as the directive rule of human conduct. But it is by no means an indispensable condition to the acceptance of the utilitarian standard; for that standard is not the agent's own greatest happiness, but the greatest amount of happiness altogether; 5 and if it may possibly be doubted whether a noble character is always the happier for its nobleness, there can be no doubt that it makes other people happier, and that the world in general is immensely a gainer by it. Utilitarianism, therefore, could only attain its end by the general cultiva- tion of nobleness of character, even if each individual were only benefited 10 by the nobleness of others, and his own, so far as happiness is concerned, were a sheer deduction from the benefit. But the bare enunciation of such an absurdity as this last, renders refutation superfluous.

According to the Greatest Happiness Principle, as above explained, the 10 ultimate end, with reference to and for the sake of which all other things are desirable (whether we are considering our own good or that of other people), is an existence exempt as far as possible from pain, and as rich as possible in enjoyments, both in point of quantity and quality; the test of 5 quality, and the rule for measuring it against quantity, being the preference felt by those who, in their opportunities of experience, to which must be added their habits of self-consciousness and self-observation, are best fur- nished with the means of comparison. This, being, according to the utili- tarian opinion, the end of human action, is necessarily also the standard of 10 morality; which may accordingly be defined, the rules and precepts for human conduct, by the observance of which an existence such as has been described might be, to the greatest extent possible, secured to all mankind; and not to them only, but, so far as the nature of things admits, to the whole sentient creation. 15

Against this doctrine, however, arises another class of objectors, who 11 say that happiness, in any form, cannot be the rational purpose of human life and action; because, in the first place, it is unattainable: and they con- temptuously ask, What right hast thou to be happy? a question which Mr Carlyle clenches by the addition, What right, a short time ago, hadst thou 5

even *to be*? Next, they say, that men can do *without* happiness; that all noble
human beings have felt this, and could not have become noble but by
learning the lesson of Entsagen, or renunciation; which lesson, thoroughly learnt and submitted to, they affirm to be the beginning and neces-
10 sary condition of all virtue.

12   The first of these objections would go to the root of the matter were it
well founded; for if no happiness is to be had at all by human beings, the
attainment of it cannot be the end of morality, or of any rational conduct.
Though, even in that case, something might still be said for the utilitarian
5 theory; since utility includes not solely the pursuit of happiness, but the
prevention or mitigation of unhappiness; and if the former aim be
chimerical, there will be all the greater scope and more imperative need
for the latter, so long at least as mankind think fit to live, and do not take
refuge in the simultaneous act of suicide recommended under certain
10 conditions by Novalis. When, however, it is thus positively asserted to be
impossible that human life should be happy, the assertion, if not something like a verbal quibble, is at least an exaggeration. If by happiness be
meant a continuity of highly pleasurable excitement, it is evident enough
that this is impossible. A state of exalted pleasure lasts only moments, or
15 in some cases, and with some intermissions, hours or days, and is the
occasional brilliant flash of enjoyment, not its permanent and steady
flame. Of this the philosophers who have taught that happiness is the end
of life were as fully aware as those who taunt them. The happiness which
they meant was not a life of rapture; but moments of such, in an existence
20 made up of few and transitory pains, many and various pleasures, with a
decided predominance of the active over the passive, and having as the
foundation of the whole, not to expect more from life than it is capable of
bestowing. A life thus composed, to those who have been fortunate
enough to obtain it, has always appeared worthy of the name of happi-
25 ness. And such an existence is even now the lot of many, during some considerable portion of their lives. The present wretched education, and
wretched social arrangements, are the only real hindrance to its being
attainable by almost all.

13   The objectors perhaps may doubt whether human beings, if taught to
consider happiness as the end of life, would be satisfied with such a moderate share of it. But great numbers of mankind have been satisfied with
much less. The main constituents of a satisfied life appear to be two; either
5 of which by itself is often found sufficient for the purpose: tranquillity, and
excitement. With much tranquillity, many find that they can be content
with very little pleasure: with much excitement, many can reconcile them-

selves to a considerable quantity of pain. There is assuredly no inherent impossibility in enabling even the mass of mankind to unite both; since the two are so far from being incompatible that they are in natural alliance, the prolongation of either being a preparation for, and exciting a wish for, the other. It is only those in whom indolence amounts to a vice, that do not desire excitement after an interval of repose; it is only those in whom the need of excitement is a disease, that feel the tranquillity which follows excitement dull and insipid, instead of pleasurable in direct proportion to the excitement which preceded it. When people who are tolerably fortunate in their outward lot do not find in life sufficient enjoyment to make it valuable to them, the cause generally is, caring for nobody but themselves. To those who have neither public nor private affections, the excitements of life are much curtailed, and in any case dwindle in value as the time approaches when all selfish interests must be terminated by death: while those who leave after them objects of personal affection, and especially those who have also cultivated a fellow feeling with the collective interests of mankind, retain as lively an interest in life on the eve of death as in the vigour of youth and health. Next to selfishness, the principal cause which makes life unsatisfactory, is want of mental cultivation. A cultivated mind—I do not mean that of a philosopher, but any mind to which the fountains of knowledge have been opened, and which has been taught, in any tolerable degree, to exercise its faculties—finds sources of inexhaustible interest in all that surrounds it; in the objects of nature, the achievements of art, the imaginations of poetry, the incidents of history, the ways of mankind past and present, and their prospects in the future. It is possible, indeed, to become indifferent to all this, and that too without having exhausted a thousandth part of it; but only when one has had from the beginning no moral or human interest in these things, and has sought in them only the gratification of curiosity.

Now there is absolutely no reason in the nature of things why an amount of mental culture sufficient to give an intelligent interest in these objects of contemplation, should not be the inheritance of every one born in a civilized country. As little is there an inherent necessity that any human being should be a selfish egotist, devoid of every feeling or care but those which centre in his own miserable individuality. Something far superior to this is sufficiently common even now, to give ample earnest of what the human species may be made. Genuine private affections, and a sincere interest in the public good, are possible, though in unequal degrees, to every rightly brought up human being. In a world in which there is so much to interest, so much to enjoy, and so much also to correct

and improve, every one who has this moderate amount of moral and intellectual requisites is capable of an existence which may be called enviable;
and unless such a person, through bad laws, or subjection to the will of
15 others, is denied the liberty to use the sources of happiness within his
reach, he will not fail to find this enviable existence, if he escape the positive evils of life, the great sources of physical and mental suffering—such
as indigence, disease, and the unkindness, worthlessness, or premature
loss of objects of affection. The main stress of the problem lies, therefore,
20 in the contest with these calamities, from which it is a rare good fortune
entirely to escape; which, as things now are, cannot be obviated, and often
cannot be in any material degree mitigated. Yet no one whose opinion
deserves a moment's consideration can doubt that most of the great positive evils of the world are in themselves removable, and will, if human
25 affairs continue to improve, be in the end reduced within narrow limits.
Poverty, in any sense implying suffering, may be completely extinguished
by the wisdom of society, combined with the good sense and providence
of individuals. Even that most intractable of enemies, disease, may be
indefinitely reduced in dimensions by good physical and moral education,
30 and proper control of noxious influences; while the progress of science
holds out a promise for the future of still more direct conquests over this
detestable foe. And every advance in that direction relieves us from some,
not only of the chances which cut short our own lives, but, what concerns
us still more, which deprive us of those in whom our happiness is wrapt
35 up. As for vicissitudes of fortune, and other disappointments connected
with worldly circumstances, these are principally the effect either of gross
imprudence, of ill-regulated desires, or of bad or imperfect social institutions. All the grand sources, in short, of human suffering are in a great
degree, many of them almost entirely, conquerable by human care and
40 effort; and though their removal is grievously slow—though a long succession of generations will perish in the breach before the conquest is com-
pleted, and this world becomes all that, if will and knowledge were not
wanting, it might easily be made—yet every mind sufficiently intelligent
and generous to bear a part, however small and unconspicuous, in the
45 endeavour, will draw a noble enjoyment from the contest itself, which he
would not for any bribe in the form of selfish indulgence consent to be
without.

15 And this leads to the true estimation of what is said by the objectors
concerning the possibility, and the obligation, of learning to do without
happiness. Unquestionably it is possible to do without happiness; it is done
involuntarily by nineteen twentieths of mankind, even in those parts of

our present world which are least deep in barbarism; and it often has to be 5
done voluntarily by the hero or the martyr, for the sake of something
which he prizes more than his individual happiness. But this something,
what is it, unless the happiness of others, or some of the requisites of happiness? It is noble to be capable of resigning entirely one's own portion of
happiness, or chances of it: but, after all, this self-sacrifice must be for some 10
end; it is not its own end; and if we are told that its end is not happiness, but
virtue, which is better than happiness, I ask, would the sacrifice be made if
the hero or martyr did not believe that it would earn for others immunity
from similar sacrifices? Would it be made, if he thought that his renunciation of happiness for himself would produce no fruit for any of his fellow 15
creatures, but to make their lot like his, and place them also in the condition of persons who have renounced happiness? All honour to those who
can abnegate for themselves the personal enjoyment of life, when by such
renunciation they contribute worthily to increase the amount of happiness in the world; but he who does it, or professes to do it, for any other 20
purpose, is no more deserving of admiration than the ascetic mounted on
his pillar. He may be an inspiriting proof of what men *can* do, but assuredly
not an example of what they *should*.

Though it is only in a very imperfect state of the world's arrangements **16**
that any one can best serve the happiness of others by the absolute sacrifice of his own, yet so long as the world is in that imperfect state, I fully
acknowledge that the readiness to make such a sacrifice is the highest
virtue which can be found in man. I will add, that in this condition of the 5
world, paradoxical as the assertion may be, the conscious ability to do
without happiness gives the best prospect of realizing such happiness as is
attainable. For nothing except that consciousness can raise a person above
the chances of life, by making him feel that, let fate and fortune do their
worst, they have not power to subdue him: which, once felt, frees him 10
from excess of anxiety concerning the evils of life, and enables him, like
many a Stoic in the worst times of the Roman Empire, to cultivate in tranquillity the sources of satisfaction accessible to him, without concerning
himself about the uncertainty of their duration, any more than about
their inevitable end. 15

Meanwhile, let utilitarians never cease to claim the morality of self- **17**
devotion as a possession which belongs by as good a right to them, as
either to the Stoic or to the Transcendentalist. The utilitarian morality
does recognise in human beings the power of sacrificing their own greatest good for the good of others. It only refuses to admit that the sacrifice is 5
itself a good. A sacrifice which does not increase, or tend to increase, the

sum total of happiness, it considers as wasted. The only self-renunciation which it applauds, is devotion to the happiness, or to some of the means of happiness, of others; either of mankind collectively, or of individuals
10 within the limits imposed by the collective interests of mankind.

18 I must again repeat, what the assailants of utilitarianism seldom have the justice to acknowledge, that the happiness which forms the utilitarian standard of what is right in conduct, is not the agent's own happiness, but that of all concerned. As between his own happiness and that of others,
5 utilitarianism requires him to be as strictly impartial as a disinterested and benevolent spectator. In the golden rule of Jesus of Nazareth, we read the complete spirit of the ethics of utility. To do as one would be done by, and to love one's neighbour as oneself, constitute the ideal perfection of utilitarian morality. As the means of making the nearest approach to this ideal,
10 utility would enjoin, first, that laws and social arrangements should place the happiness, or (as speaking practically it may be called) the interest, of every individual, as nearly as possible in harmony with the interest of the whole; and secondly, that education and opinion, which have so vast a power over human character, should so use that power as to establish in
15 the mind of every individual an indissoluble association between his own happiness and the good of the whole; especially between his own happiness and the practice of such modes of conduct, negative and positive, as regard for the universal happiness prescribes: so that not only he may be unable to conceive the possibility of happiness to himself, consistently
20 with conduct opposed to the general good, but also that a direct impulse to promote the general good may be in every individual one of the habitual motives of action, and the sentiments connected therewith may fill a large and prominent place in every human being's sentient existence. If the impugners of the utilitarian morality represented it to their own minds in
25 this its true character, I know not what recommendation possessed by any other morality they could possibly affirm to be wanting to it: what more beautiful or more exalted developments of human nature any other ethical system can be supposed to foster, or what springs of action, not accessible to the utilitarian, such systems rely on for giving effect to their
30 mandates.

19 The objectors to utilitarianism cannot always be charged with representing it in a discreditable light. On the contrary, those among them who entertain anything like a just idea of its disinterested character, sometimes find fault with its standard as being too high for humanity. They say it is
5 exacting too much to require that people shall always act from the inducement of promoting the general interests of society. But this is to mistake

the very meaning of a standard of morals, and to confound the rule of action with the motive of it. It is the business of ethics to tell us what are our duties, or by what test we may know them; but no system of ethics requires that the sole motive of all we do shall be a feeling of duty; on the contrary, ninety-nine hundredths of all our actions are done from other motives, and rightly so done, if the rule of duty does not condemn them. It is the more unjust to utilitarianism that this particular misapprehension should be made a ground of objection to it, inasmuch as utilitarian moralists have gone beyond almost all others in affirming that the motive has nothing to do with the morality of the action, though much with the worth of the agent. He who saves a fellow creature from drowning does what is morally right, whether his motive be duty, or the hope of being paid for his trouble: he who betrays the friend that trusts him, is guilty of a crime, even if his object be to serve another friend to whom he is under greater obligations.* But to speak only of actions done from the motive of duty, and in direct obedience to principle: it is a misapprehension of the utilitarian mode of thought, to conceive it as implying that people should fix their minds upon so wide a generality as the world, or society at large. The great majority of good actions are intended, not for the benefit of the world, but for that of individuals, of which the good of the world is made up; and the thoughts of the most virtuous man need not on these

* An opponent, whose intellectual and moral fairness it is a pleasure to acknowledge (the Rev. J. Llewellyn Davies), has objected to this passage, saying, "Surely the rightness or wrongness of saving a man from drowning does depend very much upon the motive with which it is done. Suppose that a tyrant, when his enemy jumped into the sea to escape from him, saved him from drowning simply in order that he might inflict upon him more exquisite tortures, would it tend to clearness to speak of that rescue as 'a morally right action?' Or suppose again, according to one of the stock illustrations of ethical inquiries, that a man betrayed a trust received from a friend, because the discharge of it would fatally injure that friend himself or some one belonging to him, would utilitarianism compel one to call the betrayal 'a crime' as much as if it had been done from the meanest motive?"

I submit, that he who saves another from drowning in order to kill him by torture afterwards, does not differ only in motive from him who does the same thing from duty or benevolence; the act itself is different. The rescue of the man is, in the case supposed, only the necessary first step of an act far more atrocious than leaving him to drown would have been. Had Mr Davies said, "The rightness or wrongness of saving a man from drowning does depend very much"—not upon the motive, but—"upon the *intention*," no utilitarian would have differed from him. Mr Davies, by an oversight too common not to be quite venial, has in this case confounded the very different ideas of Motive and Intention. There is no point which utilitarian thinkers (and Bentham pre-eminently) have taken more pains to illustrate than this. The morality of the action depends entirely upon the intention—that is, upon what the agent *wills to do*. But the motive, that is, the feeling which makes him will so to do, when it makes no difference in the act, makes none in the morality: though it makes a great difference in our moral estimation of the agent, especially if it indicates a good or a bad habitual *disposition*—a bent of character from which useful, or from which hurtful actions are likely to arise.

occasions travel beyond the particular persons concerned, except so far as is necessary to assure himself that in benefiting them he is not violating
30 the rights—that is, the legitimate and authorized expectations—of any one else. The multiplication of happiness is, according to the utilitarian ethics, the object of virtue: the occasions on which any person (except one in a thousand) has it in his power to do this on an extended scale, in other words, to be a public benefactor, are but exceptional; and on these occa-
35 sions alone is he called on to consider public utility; in every other case, private utility, the interest or happiness of some few persons, is all he has to attend to. Those alone the influence of whose actions extends to society in general, need concern themselves habitually about so large an object. In the case of abstinences indeed—of things which people forbear to do,
40 from moral considerations, though the consequences in the particular case might be beneficial—it would be unworthy of an intelligent agent not to be consciously aware that the action is of a class which, if practised generally, would be generally injurious, and that this is the ground of the obligation to abstain from it. The amount of regard for the public interest
45 implied in this recognition, is no greater than is demanded by every system of morals; for they all enjoin to abstain from whatever is manifestly perni-cious to society.

20   The same considerations dispose of another reproach against the doc-trine of utility, founded on a still grosser misconception of the purpose of a standard of morality, and of the very meaning of the words right and wrong. It is often affirmed that utilitarianism renders men cold and
5 unsympathizing; that it chills their moral feelings towards individuals; that it makes them regard only the dry and hard consideration of the conse-quences of actions, not taking into their moral estimate the qualities from which those actions emanate. If the assertion means that they do not allow their judgment respecting the rightness or wrongness of an action to be
10 influenced by their opinion of the qualities of the person who does it, this is a complaint not against utilitarianism, but against having any standard of morality at all; for certainly no known ethical standard decides an action to be good or bad because it is done by a good or a bad man, still less because done by an amiable, a brave, or a benevolent man, or the contrary. These
15 considerations are relevant, not to the estimation of actions, but of persons; and there is nothing in the utilitarian theory inconsistent with the fact that there are other things which interest us in persons besides the rightness and wrongness of their actions. The Stoics, indeed, with the paradoxical misuse of language which was part of their system, and by
20 which they strove to raise themselves above all concern about anything

but virtue, were fond of saying that he who has that has everything; that he, and only he, is rich, is beautiful, is a king. But no claim of this description is made for the virtuous man by the utilitarian doctrine. Utilitarians are quite aware that there are other desirable possessions and qualities besides virtue, and are perfectly willing to allow to all of them their full 25 worth. They are also aware that a right action does not necessarily indicate a virtuous character, and that actions which are blameable often proceed from qualities entitled to praise. When this is apparent in any particular case, it modifies their estimation, not certainly of the act, but of the agent. I grant that they are, notwithstanding, of opinion, that in the long run the 30 best proof of a good character is good actions; and resolutely refuse to consider any mental disposition as good, of which the predominant tendency is to produce bad conduct. This makes them unpopular with many people; but it is an unpopularity which they must share with every one who regards the distinction between right and wrong in a serious light; 35 and the reproach is not one which a conscientious utilitarian need be anxious to repel.

If no more be meant by the objection than that many utilitarians look 21 on the morality of actions, as measured by the utilitarian standard, with too exclusive a regard, and do not lay sufficient stress upon the other beauties of character which go towards making a human being lovable or admirable, this may be admitted. Utilitarians who have cultivated their 5 moral feelings, but not their sympathies nor their artistic perceptions, do fall into this mistake; and so do all other moralists under the same conditions. What can be said in excuse for other moralists is equally available for them, namely, that if there is to be any error, it is better that it should be on that side. As a matter of fact, we may affirm that among utilitarians as 10 among adherents of other systems, there is every imaginable degree of rigidity and of laxity in the application of their standard: some are even puritanically rigorous, while others are as indulgent as can possibly be desired by sinner or by sentimentalist. But on the whole, a doctrine which brings prominently forward the interest that mankind have in the repres- 15 sion and prevention of conduct which violates the moral law, is likely to be inferior to no other in turning the sanctions of opinion against such violations. It is true, the question, What does violate the moral law? is one on which those who recognise different standards of morality are likely now and then to differ. But difference of opinion on moral questions was not 20 first introduced into the world by utilitarianism, while that doctrine does supply, if not always an easy, at all events a tangible and intelligible mode of deciding such differences.

22   It may not be superfluous to notice a few more of the common misap-
prehensions of utilitarian ethics, even those which are so obvious and
gross that it might appear impossible for any person of candour and intelligence to fall into them: since persons, even of considerable mental
5   endowments, often give themselves so little trouble to understand the
bearings of any opinion against which they entertain a prejudice, and men
are in general so little conscious of this voluntary ignorance as a defect,
that the vulgarest misunderstandings of ethical doctrines are continually
met with in the deliberate writings of persons of the greatest pretensions
10   both to high principle and to philosophy. We not uncommonly hear the
doctrine of utility inveighed against as a *godless* doctrine. If it be necessary
to say anything at all against so mere an assumption, we may say that the
question depends upon what idea we have formed of the moral character
of the Deity. If it be a true belief that God desires, above all things, the hap-
15   piness of his creatures, and that this was his purpose in their creation,
utility is not only not a godless doctrine, but more profoundly religious
than any other. If it be meant that utilitarianism does not recognise the
revealed will of God as the supreme law of morals, I answer, that an utilitarian who believes in the perfect goodness and wisdom of God, necessar-
20   ily believes that whatever God has thought fit to reveal on the subject of
morals, must fulfil the requirements of utility in a supreme degree. But
others besides utilitarians have been of opinion that the Christian revelation was intended, and is fitted, to inform the hearts and minds of
mankind with a spirit whi h should enable them to find for themselves
25   what is right, and incline them to do it when found, rather than to tell
them, except in a very general way, what it is: and that we need a doctrine
of ethics, carefully followed out, to *interpret* to us the will of God. Whether
this opinion is correct or not, it is superfluous here to discuss; since
whatever aid religion, either natural or revealed, can afford to ethical inves-
30   tigation, is as open to the utilitarian moralist as to any other. He can use it
as the testimony of God to the usefulness or hurtfulness of any given
course of action, by as good a right as others can use it for the indication
of a transcendental law, having no connexion with usefulness or with
happiness.

23   Again, Utility is often summarily stigmatized as an immoral doctrine by
giving it the name of Expediency, and taking advantage of the popular use
of that term to contrast it with Principle. But the Expedient, in the sense in
which it is opposed to the Right, generally means that which is expedient
5   for the particular interest of the agent himself; as when a minister sacrifices the interest of his country to keep himself in place. When it means

anything better than this, it means that which is expedient for some immediate object, some temporary purpose, but which violates a rule whose observance is expedient in a much higher degree. The Expedient, in this sense, instead of being the same thing with the useful, is a branch of the hurtful. Thus, it would often be expedient, for the purpose of getting over some momentary embarrassment, or attaining some object immediately useful to ourselves or others, to tell a lie. But inasmuch as the cultivation in ourselves of a sensitive feeling on the subject of veracity, is one of the most useful, and the enfeeblement of that feeling one of the most hurtful, things to which our conduct can be instrumental; and inasmuch as any, even unintentional, deviation from truth does that much towards weakening the trustworthiness of human assertion, which is not only the principal support of all present social well-being, but the insufficiency of which does more than any one thing that can be named to keep back civilization, virtue, everything on which human happiness on the largest scale depends; we feel that the violation, for a present advantage, of a rule of such transcendant expediency, is not expedient, and that he who, for the sake of a convenience to himself or to some other individual, does what depends on him to deprive mankind of the good, and inflict upon them the evil, involved in the greater or less reliance which they can place in each other's word, acts the part of one of their worst enemies. Yet that even this rule, sacred as it is, admits of possible exceptions, is acknowledged by all moralists; the chief of which is when the withholding of some fact (as of information from a malefactor, or of bad news from a person dangerously ill) would preserve some one (especially a person other than oneself) from great and unmerited evil, and when the withholding can only be effected by denial. But in order that the exception may not extend itself beyond the need, and may have the least possible effect in weakening reliance on veracity, it ought to be recognised, and, if possible, its limits defined; and if the principle of utility is good for anything, it must be good for weighing these conflicting utilities against one another, and marking out the region within which one or the other preponderates.

Again, defenders of utility often find themselves called upon to reply to such objections as this—that there is not time, previous to action, for calculating and weighing the effects of any line of conduct on the general happiness. This is exactly as if any one were to say that it is impossible to guide our conduct by Christianity, because there is not time, on every occasion on which anything has to be done, to read through the Old and New Testaments. The answer to the objection is, that there has been ample time, namely, the whole past duration of the human species.

During all that time mankind have been learning by experience the tendencies of actions; on which experience all the prudence, as well as all the
morality of life, is dependent. People talk as if the commencement of this
course of experience had hitherto been put off, and as if, at the moment
when some man feels tempted to meddle with the property or life of
another, he had to begin considering for the first time whether murder and
theft are injurious to human happiness. Even then I do not think that he
would find the question very puzzling; but, at all events, the matter is now
done to his hand. It is truly a whimsical supposition that if mankind were
agreed in considering utility to be the test of morality, they would remain
without any agreement as to what *is* useful, and would take no measures
for having their notions on the subject taught to the young, and enforced
by law and opinion. There is no difficulty in proving any ethical standard
whatever to work ill, if we suppose universal idiocy to be conjoined with it;
but on any hypothesis short of that, mankind must by this time have
acquired positive beliefs as to the effects of some actions on their happiness; and the beliefs which have thus come down are the rules of morality
for the multitude, and for the philosopher until he has succeeded in finding
better. That philosophers might easily do this, even now, on many subjects; that the received code of ethics is by no means of divine right; and
that mankind have still much to learn as to the effects of actions on the
general happiness, I admit, or rather, earnestly maintain. The corollaries
from the principle of utility, like the precepts of every practical art, admit
of indefinite improvement, and, in a progressive state of human mind,
their improvement is perpetually going on. But to consider the rules of
morality as improvable, is one thing; to pass over the intermediate generalizations entirely, and endeavour to test each individual action directly by
the first principle, is another. It is a strange notion that the acknowledg-
ment of a first principle is inconsistent with the admission of secondary
ones. To inform a traveller respecting the place of his ultimate destination,
is not to forbid the use of landmarks and direction-posts on the way. The
proposition that happiness is the end and aim of morality, does not mean
that no road ought to be laid down to that goal, or that persons going
thither should not be advised to take one direction rather than another.
Men really ought to leave off talking a kind of nonsense on this subject,
which they would neither talk nor listen to on other matters of practical
concernment. Nobody argues that the art of navigation is not founded
on astronomy, because sailors cannot wait to calculate the Nautical
Almanack. Being rational creatures, they go to sea with it ready calculated;
and all rational creatures go out upon the sea of life with their minds made

up on the common questions of right and wrong, as well as on many of
the far more difficult questions of wise and foolish. And this, as long as 50
foresight is a human quality, it is to be presumed they will continue to do.
Whatever we adopt as the fundamental principle of morality, we require
subordinate principles to apply it by: the impossibility of doing without
them, being common to all systems, can afford no argument against any
one in particular: but gravely to argue as if no such secondary principles 55
could be had, and as if mankind had remained till now, and always must
remain, without drawing any general conclusions from the experience of
human life, is as high a pitch, I think, as absurdity has ever reached in philosophical controversy.

The remainder of the stock arguments against utilitarianism mostly **25**
consist in laying to its charge the common infirmities of human nature,
and the general difficulties which embarrass conscientious persons in
shaping their course through life. We are told that an utilitarian will be apt
to make his own particular case an exception to moral rules, and, when 5
under temptation, will see an utility in the breach of a rule, greater than
he will see in its observance. But is utility the only creed which is able to
furnish us with excuses for evil doing, and means of cheating our own conscience? They are afforded in abundance by all doctrines which recognise
as a fact in morals the existence of conflicting considerations; which all 10
doctrines do, that have been believed by sane persons. It is not the fault of
any creed, but of the complicated nature of human affairs, that rules of
conduct cannot be so framed as to require no exceptions, and that hardly
any kind of action can safely be laid down as either always obligatory or
always condemnable. There is no ethical creed which does not temper the 15
rigidity of its laws, by giving a certain latitude, under the moral responsibility of the agent, for accommodation to peculiarities of circumstances;
and under every creed, at the opening thus made, self-deception and dis-
honest casuistry get in. There exists no moral system under which there
do not arise unequivocal cases of conflicting obligation. These are the real 20
difficulties, the knotty points both in the theory of ethics, and in the conscientious guidance of personal conduct. They are overcome practically
with greater or with less success according to the intellect and virtue of
the individual; but it can hardly be pretended that anyone will be the less
qualified for dealing with them, from possessing an ultimate standard to 25
which conflicting rights and duties can be referred. If utility is the ultimate
source of moral obligations, utility may be invoked to decide between
them when their demands are incompatible. Though the application of
the standard may be difficult, it is better than none at all: while in other

30 systems, the moral laws all claiming independent authority, there is no
common umpire entitled to interfere between them; their claims to precedence one over another rest on little better than sophistry, and unless
determined, as they generally are, by the unacknowledged influence of
considerations of utility, afford a free scope for the actions of personal
35 desires and partialities. We must remember that only in these cases of conflict between secondary principles is it requisite that first principles should
be appealed to. There is no case of moral obligation in which some secondary principle is not involved; and if only one, there can seldom be any
real doubt which one it is in the mind of any person by whom the principle
40 itself is recognised.

3

OF THE ULTIMATE SANCTION OF
THE PRINCIPLE OF UTILITY.

THE question is often asked, and properly so, in regard to any supposed 1
moral standard—What is its sanction? what are the motives to obey it?
or more specifically, what is the source of its obligation? whence does it
derive its binding force? It is a necessary part of moral philosophy to
provide the answer to this question; which, though frequently assuming 5
the shape of an objection to the utilitarian morality, as if it had some
special applicability to that above others, really arises in regard to all standards. It arises, in fact, whenever a person is called on to *adopt* a standard,
or refer morality to any basis on which he has not been accustomed to rest
it. For the customary morality, that which education and opinion have 10
consecrated, is the only one which presents itself to the mind with the
feeling of being *in itself* obligatory; and when a person is asked to believe
that this morality *derives* its obligation from some general principle round
which custom has not thrown the same halo, the assertion is to him a
paradox; the supposed corollaries seem to have a more binding force than 15
the original theorem; the superstructure seems to stand better without,
than with, what is represented as its foundation. He says to himself, I feel
that I am bound not to rob or murder, betray or deceive; but why am I
bound to promote the general happiness? If my own happiness lies in
something else, why may I not give that the preference? 20

If the view adopted by the utilitarian philosophy of the nature of the 2
moral sense be correct, this difficulty will always present itself, until the
influences which form moral character have taken the same hold of
the principle which they have taken of some of the consequences—until,
by the improvement of education, the feeling of unity with our fellow 5
creatures shall be (what it cannot be doubted that Christ intended it to be)
as deeply rooted in our character, and to our own consciousness as completely a part of our nature, as the horror of crime is in an ordinarily
well-brought up young person. In the mean time, however, the difficulty

10 has no peculiar application to the doctrine of utility, but is inherent in every attempt to analyse morality and reduce it to principles; which, unless the principle is already in men's minds invested with as much sacredness as any of its applications, always seems to divest them of a part of their sanctity.

3   The principle of utility either has, or there is no reason why it might not have, all the sanctions which belong to any other system of morals. Those sanctions are either external or internal. Of the external sanctions it is not necessary to speak at any length. They are, the hope of favour and the fear

5 of displeasure from our fellow creatures or from the Ruler of the Universe, along with whatever we may have of sympathy or affection for them, or of love and awe of Him, inclining us to do his will independently of selfish consequences. There is evidently no reason why all these motives for observance should not attach themselves to the utilitarian morality, as

10 completely and as powerfully as to any other. Indeed, those of them which refer to our fellow creatures are sure to do so, in proportion to the amount of general intelligence; for whether there be any other ground of moral obligation than the general happiness or not, men do desire happiness; and however imperfect may be their own practice, they desire and commend

15 all conduct in others towards themselves, by which they think their happiness is promoted. With regard to the religious motive, if men believe, as most profess to do, in the goodness of God, those who think that conduciveness to the general happiness is the essence, or even only the criterion, of good, must necessarily believe that it is also that which God

20 approves. The whole force therefore of external reward and punishment, whether physical or moral, and whether proceeding from God or from our fellow men, together with all that the capacities of human nature admit, of disinterested devotion to either, become available to enforce the utilitarian morality, in proportion as the morality is recognised; and the

25 more powerfully, the more the appliances of education and general cultivation are bent to the purpose.

4   So far as to external sanctions. The internal sanction of duty, whatever our standard of duty may be, is one and the same—a feeling in our own mind; a pain, more or less intense, attendant on violation of duty, which in properly-cultivated moral natures rises, in the more serious cases, into

5 shrinking from it as an impossibility. This feeling, when disinterested, and connecting itself with the pure idea of duty, and not with some particular form of it, or with any of the merely **accessory** circumstances, is the essence of Conscience; though in that complex phenomenon as it actually exists, the simple fact is in general all encrusted over with collateral associ-

ations, derived from sympathy, from love, and still more from fear; from all ₁₀
the forms of religious feeling; from the recollections of childhood and of
all our past life; from self-esteem, desire of the esteem of others, and occasionally even self-abasement. This extreme complication is, I apprehend,
the origin of the sort of mystical character which, by a tendency of the
human mind of which there are many other examples, is apt to be attrib- ₁₅
uted to the idea of moral obligation, and which leads people to believe
that the idea cannot possibly attach itself to any other objects than those
which, by a supposed mysterious law, are found in our present experience
to excite it. Its binding force, however, consists in the existence of a mass
of feeling which must be broken through in order to do what violates our ₂₀
standard of right, and which, if we do nevertheless violate that standard,
will probably have to be encountered afterwards in the form of remorse.
Whatever theory we have of the nature or origin of conscience, this is
what essentially constitutes it.

The ultimate sanction, therefore, of all morality (external motives 5
apart) being a subjective feeling in our own minds, I see nothing embar-
rassing to those whose standard is utility, in the question, what is the sanction of that particular standard? We may answer, the same as of all other
moral standards—the conscientious feelings of mankind. Undoubtedly ₅
this sanction has no binding efficacy on those who do not possess the feelings it appeals to; but neither will these persons be more obedient to any
other moral principle than to the utilitarian one. On them morality of any
kind has no hold but through the external sanctions. Meanwhile the feelings exist, a fact in human nature, the reality of which, and the great power ₁₀
with which they are capable of acting on those in whom they have been
duly cultivated, are proved by experience. No reason has ever been shown
why they may not be cultivated to as great intensity in connexion with the
utilitarian, as with any other rule of morals.

There is, I am aware, a disposition to believe that a person who sees in 6
moral obligation a transcendental fact, an objective reality belonging to
the province of 'Things in themselves,' is likely to be more obedient to it
than one who believes it to be entirely subjective, having its seat in human
consciousness only. But whatever a person's opinion may be on this point ₅
of Ontology, the force he is really urged by is his own subjective feeling,
and is exactly measured by its strength. No one's belief that Duty is an
objective reality is stronger than the belief that God is so; yet the belief in
God, apart from the expectation of actual reward and punishment, only
operates on conduct through, and in proportion to, the subjective reli- ₁₀
gious feeling. The sanction, so far as it is disinterested, is always in the

mind itself; and the notion therefore of the transcendental moralists must be, that this sanction will not exist *in* the mind unless it is believed to have its root out of the mind; and that if a person is able to say to himself, This

15 which is restraining me, and which is called my conscience, is only a feeling in my own mind, he may possibly draw the conclusion that when the feeling ceases the obligation ceases, and that if he find the feeling inconvenient, he may disregard it, and endeavour to get rid of it. But is this danger confined to the utilitarian morality? Does the belief that moral

20 obligation has its seat outside the mind make the feeling of it too strong to be got rid of? The fact is so far otherwise, that all moralists admit and lament the ease with which, in the generality of minds, conscience can be silenced or stifled. The question, Need I obey my conscience? is quite as often put to themselves by persons who never heard of the principle of

25 utility, as by its adherents. Those whose conscientious feelings are so weak as to allow of their asking this question, if they answer it affirmatively, will not do so because they believe in the transcendental theory, but because of the external sanctions.

7   It is not necessary, for the present purpose, to decide whether the feeling of duty is innate or implanted. Assuming it to be innate, it is an open question to what objects it naturally attaches itself; for the philosophic supporters of that theory are now agreed that the intuitive perception is of

5 principles of morality, and not of the details. If there be anything innate in the matter, I see no reason why the feeling which is innate should not be that of regard to the pleasures and pains of others. If there is any principle of morals which is intuitively obligatory, I should say it must be that. If so, the intuitive ethics would coincide with the utilitarian, and there

10 would be no further quarrel between them. Even as it is, the intuitive moralists, though they believe that there are other intuitive moral obligations, do already believe this to be one; for they unanimously hold that a large *portion* of morality turns upon the consideration due to the interests of our fellow creatures. Therefore, if the belief in the transcendental

15 origin of moral obligation gives any additional efficacy to the internal sanction, it appears to me that the utilitarian principle has already the benefit of it.

8   On the other hand, if, as is my own belief, the moral feelings are not innate, but acquired, they are not for that reason the less natural. It is natural to man to speak, to reason, to build cities, to cultivate the ground, though these are acquired faculties. The moral feelings are not indeed a

5 part of our nature, in the sense of being in any perceptible degree present in all of us; but this, unhappily, is a fact admitted by those who believe the

most strenuously in their transcendental origin. Like the other acquired capacities above referred to, the moral faculty, if not a part of our nature, is a natural outgrowth from it; capable, like them, in a certain small degree, of springing up spontaneously; and susceptible of being brought by culti- 10 vation to a high degree of development. Unhappily it is also susceptible, by a sufficient use of the external sanctions and of the force of early impressions, of being cultivated in almost any direction: so that there is hardly anything so absurd or so mischievous that it may not, by means of these influences, be made to act on the human mind with all the authority of 15 conscience. To doubt that the same potency might be given by the same means to the principle of utility, even if it had no foundation in human nature, would be flying in the face of all experience.

But moral associations which are wholly of artificial creation, when 9 intellectual culture goes on, yield by degrees to the dissolving force of analysis: and if the feeling of duty, when associated with utility, would appear equally arbitrary; if there were no leading department of our nature, no powerful class of sentiments, with which that association 5 would harmonize, which would make us feel it congenial, and incline us not only to foster it in others (for which we have abundant interested motives), but also to cherish it in ourselves; if there were not, in short, a natural basis of sentiment for utilitarian morality, it might well happen that this association also, even after it had been implanted by education, 10 might be analysed away.

But there *is* this basis of powerful natural sentiment; and this it is which, 10 when once the general happiness is recognised as the ethical standard, will constitute the strength of the utilitarian morality. This firm foundation is that of the social feelings of mankind; the desire to be in unity with our fellow creatures, which is already a powerful principle in human nature, 5 and happily one of those which tend to become stronger, even without express inculcation, from the influences of advancing civilization. The social state is at once so natural, so necessary, and so habitual to man, that, except in some unusual circumstances or by an effort of voluntary abstraction, he never conceives himself otherwise than as a member of a body; 10 and this association is riveted more and more, as mankind are further removed from the state of savage independence. Any condition, therefore, which is essential to a state of society, becomes more and more an inseparable part of every person's conception of the state of things which he is born into, and which is the destiny of a human being. Now, society 15 between human beings, except in the relation of master and slave, is manifestly impossible on any other footing than that the interests of all are to be consulted. Society between equals can only exist on the understanding that the interests of all are to be regarded equally. And since in all states of civilization, every person, except an absolute monarch, has equals, every one is obliged to live on these terms with somebody; and in every age some advance is made towards a state in which it will be impossible to live permanently on other terms with anybody. In this way people grow up unable to conceive as possible to them a state of total disregard of other people's interests. They are under a necessity of conceiving themselves as at least abstaining from all the grosser injuries, and (if only for their own protection) living in a state of constant protest against them. They are also familiar with the fact of co-operating with others, and proposing to themselves a collective, not an individual, interest, as the aim (at least for the time being) of their actions. So long as they are co-operating, their ends are identified with those of others; there is at least a temporary feeling that the interests of others are their own interests. Not only does all strengthening of social ties, and all healthy growth of society, give to each individual a stronger personal interest in practically consulting the welfare of others; it also leads him to identify his *feelings* more and more with their good, or at least with an ever greater degree of practical consideration for it. He comes, as though instinctively, to be conscious of himself as a being who *of course* pays regard to others. The good of others becomes to him a thing naturally and necessarily to be attended to, like any of the physical conditions of our existence. Now, whatever amount of this feeling a person has, he is urged by the strongest motives both of interest and of sympathy to demonstrate it, and to the utmost of his power encourage it in others; and even if he has none of it himself, he is as greatly interested as anyone else that others should have it. Consequently, the smallest germs of the feeling are laid hold of and nourished by the contagion of sympathy and the influences of education; and a complete web of corroborative association is woven round it, by the powerful agency of the external sanctions. This mode of conceiving ourselves and human life, as civilization goes on, is felt to be more and more natural. Every step in political improvement renders it more so, by removing the sources of opposition of interest, and levelling those inequalities of legal privilege between individuals or classes, owing to which there are large portions of mankind whose happiness it is still practicable to disregard. In an improving state of the human mind, the influences are constantly on the increase, which tend to generate in each individual a feeling of unity with all the rest; which feeling, if perfect, would make him never think of, or desire, any beneficial condition for himself, in the benefits of which they are not included. If we now suppose this feeling of unity to be taught as a religion, and the whole force of education, of institutions, and of opinion, directed, as it once was in the case of religion, to make every person grow up from infancy surrounded on all 60 sides both by the profession and by the practice of it, I think that no one, who can realize this conception, will feel any misgiving about the sufficiency of the ultimate sanction for the Happiness morality. To any ethical student who finds the realization difficult, I recommend, as a means of facilitating it, the second of M. Comte's two principal works, the *Systême* 65 *de Politique Positive.* I entertain the strongest objections to the system of politics and morals set forth in that treatise; but I think it has superabundantly shown the possibility of giving to the service of humanity, even without the aid of belief in a Providence, both the psychical power and the social efficacy of a religion; making it take hold of human life, and 70 colour all thought, feeling and action in a manner of which the greatest ascendancy ever exercised by any religion may be but a type and foretaste; and of which the danger is, not that it should be insufficient, but that it should be so excessive as to interfere unduly with human freedom and individuality. 75

Neither is it necessary to the feeling which constitutes the binding force II of the utilitarian morality on those who recognise it, to wait for those social influences which would make its obligation felt by mankind at large. In the comparatively early state of human advancement in which we now live, a person cannot indeed feel that entireness of sympathy with all 5 others, which would make any real discordance in the general direction of their conduct in life impossible; but already a person in whom the social feeling is at all developed, cannot bring himself to think of the rest of his fellow creatures as struggling rivals with him for the means of happiness, whom he must desire to see defeated in their object in order that he may 10 succeed in his. The deeply-rooted conception which every individual even now has of himself as a social being, tends to make him feel it one of his natural wants that there should be harmony between his feelings and aims and those of his fellow creatures. If differences of opinion and of mental culture make it impossible for him to share many of their actual feelings— 15 perhaps make him denounce and defy those feelings—he still needs to be conscious that his real aim and theirs do not conflict; that he is not opposing himself to what they really wish for, namely, their own good, but is, on the contrary, promoting it. This feeling in most individuals is much inferior in strength to their selfish feelings, and is often wanting altogether. But 20 to those who have it, it possesses all the characters of a natural feeling. It does not present itself to their minds as a superstition of education, or a

law despotically imposed by the power of society, but as an attribute which it would not be well for them to be without. This conviction is the ultimate
25 sanction of the greatest-happiness morality. This it is which makes any mind, of well-developed feelings, work with, and not against, the outward motives to care for others, afforded by what I have called the external sanctions; and when those sanctions are wanting, or act in an opposite direction, constitutes in itself a powerful internal binding force, in proportion
30 to the sensitiveness and thoughtfulness of the character; since few but those whose mind is a moral blank, could bear to lay out their course of life on the plan of paying no regard to others except so far as their own private interest compels.

4

OF WHAT SORT OF PROOF THE PRINCIPLE OF UTILITY IS SUSCEPTIBLE.

It has already been remarked, that questions of ultimate ends do not **1** admit of proof, in the ordinary acceptation of the term. To be incapable of proof by reasoning is common to all first principles; to the first premises of our knowledge, as well as to those of our conduct. But the former, being matters of fact, may be the subject of a direct appeal to the faculties which **5** judge of fact—namely, our senses, and our internal consciousness. Can an appeal be made to the same faculties on questions of practical ends? Or by what other faculty is cognizance taken of them?

Questions about ends are, in other words, questions what things are **2** desirable. The utilitarian doctrine is, that happiness is desirable, and the only thing desirable, as an end; all other things being only desirable as means to that end. What ought to be required of this doctrine—what conditions is it requisite that the doctrine should fulfil—to make good its claim **5** to be believed?

The only proof capable of being given that an object is visible, is that **3** people actually see it. The only proof that a sound is audible, is that people hear it: and so of the other sources of our experience. In like manner, I apprehend, the sole evidence it is possible to produce that anything is desirable, is that people do actually desire it. If the end which the utili- **5** tarian doctrine proposes to itself were not, in theory and in practice, acknowledged to be an end, nothing could ever convince any person that it was so. No reason can be given why the general happiness is desirable, except that each person, so far as he believes it to be attainable, desires his own happiness. This, however, being a fact, we have not only all the proof **10** which the case admits of, but all which it is possible to require, that happiness is a good: that each person's happiness is a good to that person, and the general happiness, therefore, a good to the aggregate of all persons.

Happiness has made out its title as *one* of the ends of conduct, and conse-
15 quently one of the criteria of morality.

4   But it has not, by this alone, proved itself to be the sole criterion. To do
that, it would seem, by the same rule, necessary to show, not only that
people desire happiness, but that they never desire anything else. Now it is
palpable that they do desire things which, in common language, are decid-
5 edly distinguished from happiness. They desire, for example, virtue and
the absence of vice, no less really than pleasure and the absence of pain.
The desire of virtue is not as universal, but it is as authentic a fact, as the
desire of happiness. And hence the opponents of the utilitarian standard
deem that they have a right to infer that there are other ends of human
10 action besides happiness, and that happiness is not the standard of appro-
bation and disapprobation.

5   But does the utilitarian doctrine deny that people desire virtue, or maintain that virtue is not a thing to be desired? The very reverse. It maintains
not only that virtue is to be desired, but that it is to be desired disinterest-
edly, for itself. Whatever may be the opinion of utilitarian moralists as to
5 the original conditions by which virtue is made virtue; however they may
believe (as they do) that actions and dispositions are only virtuous because
they promote another end than virtue; yet this being granted, and it
having been decided, from considerations of this description, what *is* virtuous, they not only place virtue at the very head of the things which are
10 good as means to the ultimate end, but they also recognise as a psychological fact the possibility of its being, to the individual, a good in itself,
without looking to any end beyond it; and hold, that the mind is not in
a right state, not in a state conformable to Utility, not in the state most
conducive to the general happiness, unless it does love virtue in this
15 manner—as a thing desirable in itself, even although, in the individual
instance, it should not produce those other desirable consequences which
it tends to produce, and on account of which it is held to be virtue. This
opinion is not, in the smallest degree, a departure from the Happiness
principle. The ingredients of happiness are very various, and each of them
20 is desirable in itself, and not merely when considered as swelling an aggregate. The principle of utility does not mean that any given pleasure, as
music, for instance, or any given exemption from pain, as for example
health, are to be looked upon as means to a collective something termed
happiness, and to be desired on that account. They are desired and desir-
25 able in and for themselves; besides being means, they are a part of the end.
Virtue, according to the utilitarian doctrine, is not naturally and originally

part of the end, but it is capable of becoming so; and is desired and cherished, not as a means to happiness, but as a part of their happiness.

To illustrate this farther, we may remember that virtue is not the only **6** thing, originally a means, and which if it were not a means to anything else, would be and remain indifferent, but which by association with what it is a means to, comes to be desired for itself, and that too with the utmost intensity. What, for example, shall we say of the love of money? There is 5 nothing originally more desirable about money than about any heap of glittering pebbles. Its worth is solely that of the things which it will buy; the desires for other things than itself, which it is a means of gratifying. Yet the love of money is not only one of the strongest moving forces of human life, but money is, in many cases, desired in and for itself; the desire to 10 possess it is often stronger than the desire to use it, and goes on increasing when all the desires which point to ends beyond it, to be compassed by it, are falling off. It may be then said truly, that money is desired not for the sake of an end, but as part of the end. From being a means to happiness, it has come to be itself a principal ingredient of the individual's conception 15 of happiness. The same may be said of the majority of the great objects of human life—power, for example, or fame; except that to each of these there is a certain amount of immediate pleasure annexed, which has at least the semblance of being naturally inherent in them; a thing which cannot be said of money. Still, however, the strongest natural attraction, 20 both of power and of fame, is the immense aid they give to the attainment of our other wishes; and it is the strong association thus generated between them and all our objects of desire, which gives to the direct desire of them the intensity it often assumes, so as in some characters to surpass in strength all other desires. In these cases the means have become a part of 25 the end, and a more important part of it than any of the things which they are means to. What was once desired as an instrument for the attainment of happiness, has come to be desired for its own sake. In being desired for its own sake it is, however, desired as *part* of happiness. The person is made, or thinks he would be made, happy by its mere possession; and is 30 made unhappy by failure to obtain it. The desire of it is not a different thing from the desire of happiness, any more than the love of music, or the desire of health. They are included in happiness. They are some of the elements of which the desire of happiness is made up. Happiness is not an abstract idea, but a concrete whole; and these are some of its parts. And 35 the utilitarian standard sanctions and approves their being so. Life would be a poor thing, very ill provided with sources of happiness, if there were

not this provision of nature, by which things originally indifferent, but conducive to, or otherwise associated with, the satisfaction of our primi-
40 tive desires, become in themselves sources of pleasure more valuable than the primitive pleasures, both in permanency, in the space of human exis- tence that they are capable of covering, and even in intensity.

7   Virtue, according to the utilitarian conception, is a good of this descrip- tion. There was no original desire of it, or motive to it, save its conducive- ness to pleasure, and especially to protection from pain. But through the association thus formed, it may be felt a good in itself, and desired as such
5 with as great intensity as any other good; and with this difference between it and the love of money, of power, or of fame, that all of these may, and often do, render the individual noxious to the other members of the society to which he belongs, whereas there is nothing which makes him so much a blessing to them as the cultivation of the disinterested love of
10 virtue. And consequently, the utilitarian standard, while it tolerates and approves those other acquired desires, up to the point beyond which they would be more injurious to the general happiness than promotive of it, enjoins and requires the cultivation of the love of virtue up to the greatest strength possible, as being above all things important to the general
15 happiness.

8   It results from the preceding considerations, that there is in reality nothing desired except happiness. Whatever is desired otherwise than as a means to some end beyond itself, and ultimately to happiness, is desired as itself a part of happiness, and is not desired for itself until it has become
5 so. Those who desire virtue for its own sake, desire it either because the consciousness of it is a pleasure, or because the consciousness of being without it is a pain, or for both reasons united; as in truth the pleasure and pain seldom exist separately, but almost always together, the same person feeling pleasure in the degree of virtue attained, and pain in not having
10 attained more. If one of these gave him no pleasure, and the other no pain, he would not love or desire virtue, or would desire it only for the other benefits which it might produce to himself or to persons whom he cared for.

9   We have now, then, an answer to the question, of what sort of proof the principle of utility is susceptible. If the opinion which I have now stated is psychologically true—if human nature is so constituted as to desire nothing which is not either a part of happiness or a means of happiness,
5 we can have no other proof, and we require no other, that these are the only things desirable. If so, happiness is the sole end of human action, and the promotion of it the test by which to judge of all human conduct; from

whence it necessarily follows that it must be the criterion of morality, since a part is included in the whole.

And now to decide whether this is really so; whether mankind do desire   10
nothing for itself but that which is a pleasure to them, or of which the absence is a pain; we have evidently arrived at a question of fact and experience, dependent, like all similar questions, upon evidence. It can only be determined by practised self-consciousness and self-observation, assisted   5
by observation of others. I believe that these sources of evidence, impartially consulted, will declare that desiring a thing and finding it pleasant, aversion to it and thinking of it as painful, are phenomena entirely inseparable, or rather two parts of the same phenomenon; in strictness of language, two different modes of naming the same psychological fact: that   10
to think of an object as desirable (unless for the sake of its consequences), and to think of it as pleasant, are one and the same thing; and that to desire anything, except in proportion as the idea of it is pleasant, is a physical and metaphysical impossibility.

So obvious does this appear to me, that I expect it will hardly be dis-   11
puted: and the objection made will be, not that desire can possibly be directed to anything ultimately except pleasure and exemption from pain, but that the will is a different thing from desire; that a person of confirmed virtue, or any other person whose purposes are fixed, carries out his pur-   5
poses without any thought of the pleasure he has in contemplating them, or expects to derive from their fulfilment; and persists in acting on them, even though these pleasures are much diminished, by changes in his character or decay of his passive sensibilities, or are outweighed by the pains which the pursuit of the purposes may bring upon him. All this I fully   10
admit, and have stated it elsewhere, as positively and emphatically as any one. Will, the active phenomenon, is a different thing from desire, the state of passive sensibility, and though originally an offshoot from it, may in time take root and detach itself from the parent stock; so much so, that in the case of an habitual purpose, instead of willing the thing because we   15
desire it, we often desire it only because we will it. This, however, is but an instance of that familiar fact, the power of habit, and is nowise confined to the case of virtuous actions. Many indifferent things, which men originally did from a motive of some sort, they continue to do from habit. Sometimes this is done unconsciously, the consciousness coming only   20
after the action: at other times with conscious volition, but volition which has became habitual, and is put into operation by the force of habit, in opposition perhaps to the deliberate preference, as often happens with those who have contracted habits of vicious or hurtful indulgence. Third

25 and last comes the case in which the habitual act of will in the individual instance is not in contradiction to the general intention prevailing at other times, but in fulfilment of it; as in the case of the person of confirmed virtue, and of all who pursue deliberately and consistently any determinate end. The distinction between will and desire thus understood, is an

30 authentic and highly important psychological fact; but the fact consists solely in this—that will, like all other parts of our constitution, is amenable to habit, and that we may will from habit what we no longer desire for itself, or desire only because we will it. It is not the less true that will, in the beginning, is entirely produced by desire; including in that term the

35 repelling influence of pain as well as the attractive one of pleasure. Let us take into consideration, no longer the person who has a confirmed will to do right, but him in whom that virtuous will is still feeble, conquerable by temptation, and not to be fully relied on; by what means can it be strengthened? How can the will to be virtuous, where it does not exist in sufficient

40 force, be implanted or awakened? Only by making the person *desire* virtue—by making him think of it in a pleasurable light, or of its absence in a painful one. It is by associating the doing right with pleasure, or the doing wrong with pain, or by eliciting and impressing and bringing home to the person's experience the pleasure naturally involved in the one or the

45 pain in the other, that it is possible to call forth that will to be virtuous, which, when confirmed, acts without any thought of either pleasure or pain. Will is the child of desire, and passes out of the dominion of its parent only to come under that of habit. That which is the result of habit affords no presumption of being intrinsically good; and there would be no

50 reason for wishing that the purpose of virtue should become independent of pleasure and pain, were it not that the influence of the pleasurable and painful associations which prompt to virtue is not sufficiently to be depended on for unerring constancy of action until it has acquired the support of habit. Both in feeling and in conduct, habit is the only thing

55 which imparts certainty; and it is because of the importance to others of being able to rely absolutely on one's feelings and conduct, and to oneself of being able to rely on one's own, that the will to do right ought to be cultivated into this habitual independence. In other words, this state of the will is a means to good, not intrinsically a good; and does not contradict

60 the doctrine that nothing is a good to human beings but in so far as it is either itself pleasurable, or a means of attaining pleasure or averting pain.

12　　But if this doctrine be true, the principle of utility is proved. Whether it is so or not, must now be left to the consideration of the thoughtful reader.

5

ON THE CONNEXION BETWEEN JUSTICE AND UTILITY.

In all ages of speculation, one of the strongest obstacles to the reception of **1** the doctrine that Utility or Happiness is the criterion of right and wrong, has been drawn from the idea of Justice. The powerful sentiment, and apparently clear perception, which that word recals with a rapidity and certainty resembling an instinct, have seemed to the majority of thinkers **5** to point to an inherent quality in things; to show that the Just must have an existence in Nature as something absolute—generically distinct from every variety of the Expedient, and, in idea, opposed to it, though (as is commonly acknowledged) never, in the long run, disjoined from it in fact. **10**

In the case of this, as of our other moral sentiments, there is no neces- **2** sary connexion between the question of its origin, and that of its binding force. That a feeling is bestowed on us by Nature, does not necessarily legitimate all its promptings. The feeling of justice might be a peculiar instinct, and might yet require, like our other instincts, to be controlled **5** and enlightened by a higher reason. If we have intellectual instincts, leading us to judge in a particular way, as well as animal instincts that prompt us to act in a particular way, there is no necessity that the former should be more infallible in their sphere than the latter in theirs: it may as well happen that wrong judgments are occasionally suggested by those, as **10** wrong actions by these. But though it is one thing to believe that we have natural feelings of justice, and another to acknowledge them as an ulti- mate criterion of conduct, these two opinions are very closely connected in point of fact. Mankind are always predisposed to believe that any sub- jective feeling, not otherwise accounted for, is a revelation of some objec- **15** tive reality. Our present object is to determine whether the reality, to which the feeling of justice corresponds, is one which needs any such special revelation; whether the justice or injustice of an action is a thing intrinsically peculiar, and distinct from all its other qualities, or only a

20 combination of certain of those qualities, presented under a peculiar aspect. For the purpose of this inquiry, it is practically important to consider whether the feeling itself, of justice and injustice, is *sui generis* like our sensations of colour and taste, or a derivative feeling, formed by a combination of others. And this it is the more essential to examine, as people are
25 in general willing enough to allow, that objectively the dictates of justice coincide with a part of the field of General Expediency; but inasmuch as the subjective mental feeling of Justice is different from that which commonly attaches to simple expediency, and, except in extreme cases of the latter, is far more imperative in its demands, people find it difficult to see, in
30 Justice, only a particular kind or branch of general utility, and think that its superior binding force requires a totally different origin.

3   To throw light upon this question, it is necessary to attempt to ascertain what is the distinguishing character of justice, or of injustice: what is the quality, or whether there is any quality, attributed in common to all modes of conduct designated as unjust (for justice, like many other moral attrib-
5 utes, is best defined by its opposite), and distinguishing them from such modes of conduct as are disapproved, but without having that particular epithet of disapprobation applied to them. If, in everything which men are accustomed to characterize as just or injust, some one common attribute or collection of attributes is always present, we may judge whether this
10 particular attribute or combination of attributes would be capable of gathering round it a sentiment of that peculiar character and intensity by virtue of the general laws of our emotional constitution, or whether the sentiment is inexplicable, and requires to be regarded as a special provision of Nature. If we find the former to be the case, we shall, in resolving this
15 question, have resolved also the main problem: if the latter, we shall have to seek for some other mode of investigating it.

4   To find the common attributes of a variety of objects, it is necessary to begin by surveying the objects themselves in the concrete. Let us therefore advert successively to the various modes of action, and arrangements of human affairs, which are classed, by universal or widely spread opinion, as
5 Just or as Unjust. The things well known to excite the sentiments associated with those names, are of a very multifarious character. I shall pass them rapidly in review, without studying any particular arrangement.
5   In the first place, it is mostly considered unjust to deprive any one of his personal liberty, his property, or any other thing which belongs to him by law. Here, therefore, is one instance of the application of the terms just and unjust in a perfectly definite sense, namely, that it is just to respect,

unjust to violate, the *legal rights* of anyone. But this judgment admits of 5
several exceptions, arising from the other forms in which the notions of
justice and injustice present themselves. For example, the person who
suffers the deprivation may (as the phrase is) have *forfeited* the rights
which he is so deprived of: a case to which we shall return presently. But,
also, 10

Secondly; the legal rights of which he is deprived, may be rights which **6**
ought not to have belonged to him; in other words, the law which confers
on him these rights, may be a bad law. When it is so, or when (which is the
same thing for our purpose) it is supposed to be so, opinions will differ as to
the justice or injustice of infringing it. Some maintain that no law, however 5
bad, ought to be disobeyed by an individual citizen; that his opposition to
it, if shown at all, should only be shown in endeavouring to get it altered by
competent authority. This opinion (which condemns many of the most
illustrious benefactors of mankind, and would often protect pernicious
institutions against the only weapons which, in the state of things existing 10
at the time, have any chance of succeeding against them) is defended, by
those who hold it, on grounds of expediency; principally on that of the
importance, to the common interest of mankind, of maintaining inviolate
the sentiment of submission to law. Other persons, again, hold the directly
contrary opinion, that any law, judged to be bad, may blamelessly be dis- 15
obeyed, even though it be not judged to be unjust, but only inexpedient;
while others would confine the licence of disobedience to the case of
unjust laws: but again, some say, that all laws which are inexpedient are
unjust; since every law imposes some restriction on the natural liberty of
mankind, which restriction is an injustice, unless legitimated by tending to 20
their good. Among these diversities of opinion, it seems to be universally
admitted that there may be unjust laws, and that law, consequently, is not
the ultimate criterion of justice, but may give to one person a benefit, or
impose on another an evil, which justice condemns. When, however, a law
is thought to be unjust, it seems always to be regarded as being so in the 25
same way in which a breach of law is unjust, namely, by infringing somebody's right; which, as it cannot in this case be a legal right, receives a different appellation, and is called a moral right. We may say, therefore, that a
second case of injustice consists in taking or withholding from any person
that to which he has a *moral right*. 30

Thirdly, it is universally considered just that each person should obtain **7**
that (whether good or evil) which he *deserves*; and unjust that he should
obtain a good, or be made to undergo an evil, which he does not deserve.
This is, perhaps, the clearest and most emphatic form in which the idea of

5 injustice is conceived by the general mind. As it involves the notion of desert, the question arises, what constitutes desert? Speaking in a general way, a person is understood to deserve good if he does right, evil if he does wrong; and in a more particular sense, to deserve good from those to whom he does or has done good, and evil from those to whom he does or
10 has done evil. The precept of returning good for evil has never been regarded as a case of the fulfilment of justice, but as one in which the claims of justice are waved, in obedience to other considerations.

8   Fourthly, it is confessedly unjust to *break faith* with any one: to violate an engagement, either express or implied, or disappoint expectations raised by our own conduct, at least if we have raised those expectations know-ingly and voluntarily. Like the other obligations of justice already spoken
5 of, this one is not regarded as absolute, but as capable of being overruled by a stronger obligation of justice on the other side; or by such conduct on the part of the person concerned as is deemed to absolve us from our obligation to him, and to constitute a *forfeiture* of the benefit which he has been led to expect.

9   Fifthly, it is, by universal admission, inconsistent with justice to be *partial*; to show favour or preference to one person over another, in matters to which favour and preference do not properly apply. Impartiality, however, does not seem to be regarded as a duty in itself, but rather as
5 instrumental to some other duty; for it is admitted that favour and prefer-ence are not always censurable, and indeed the cases in which they are con-demned are rather the exception than the rule. A person would be more likely to be blamed than applauded for giving his family or friends no superiority in good offices over strangers, when he could do so without
10 violating any other duty; and no one thinks it unjust to seek one person in preference to another as a friend, connexion, or companion. Impartiality where rights are concerned is of course obligatory, but this is involved in the more general obligation of giving to every one his right. A tribunal, for example, must be impartial, because it is bound to award, without regard
15 to any other consideration, a disputed object to the one of two parties who has the right to it. There are other cases in which impartiality means, being solely influenced by desert; as with those who, in the capacity of judges, preceptors, or parents, administer reward and punishment as such. There are cases, again, in which it means, being solely influenced by considera-
20 tion for the public interest; as in making a selection among candidates for a government employment. Impartiality, in short, as an obligation of justice, may be said to mean, being exclusively influenced by the consid-erations which it is supposed ought to influence the particular case in

hand; and resisting the solicitation of any motives which prompt to conduct different from what those considerations would dictate. 25

Nearly allied to the idea of impartiality, is that of *equality*; which often 10 enters as a component part both into the conception of justice and into the practice of it, and, in the eyes of many persons, constitutes its essence. But in this, still more than in any other case, the notion of justice varies in different persons, and always conforms in its variations to their notion of 5 utility. Each person maintains that equality is the dictate of justice, except where he thinks that expediency requires inequality. The justice of giving equal protection to the rights of all, is maintained by those who support the most outrageous inequality in the rights themselves. Even in slave countries it is theoretically admitted that the rights of the slave, such as 10 they are, ought to be as sacred as those of the master; and that a tribunal which fails to enforce them with equal strictness is wanting in justice; while, at the same time, institutions which leave to the slave scarcely any rights to enforce, are not deemed unjust, because they are not deemed inexpedient. Those who think that utility requires distinctions of rank, do 15 not consider it unjust that riches and social privileges should be unequally dispensed; but those who think this inequality inexpedient, think it unjust also. Whoever thinks that government is necessary, sees no injustice in as much inequality as is constituted by giving to the magistrate powers not granted to other people. Even among those who hold levelling doctrines, 20 there are as many questions of justice as there are differences of opinion about expediency. Some Communists consider it unjust that the produce of the labour of the community should be shared on any other principle than that of exact equality; others think it just that those should receive most whose needs are greatest; while others hold that those who work 25 harder, or who produce more, or whose services are more valuable to the community, may justly claim a larger quota in the division of the produce. And the sense of natural justice may be plausibly appealed to in behalf of every one of these opinions.

Among so many diverse applications of the term Justice, which yet is 11 not regarded as ambiguous, it is a matter of some difficulty to seize the mental link which holds them together, and on which the moral sentiment adhering to the term essentially depends. Perhaps, in this embarrassment, some help may be derived from the history of the word, as indicated by its 5 etymology.

In most, if not in all, languages, the etymology of the word which 12 corresponds to Just, points to an origin connected either with positive law, or with that which was in most cases the primitive form of law—

authoritative custom. *Justum* is a form of *jussum*, that which has been
ordered. *Jus* is of the same origin. Δίχαιον comes from δίχη, of which
the principal meaning, at least in the historical ages of Greece, was a suit at
law. Originally, indeed, it meant only the mode or *manner* of doing things,
but it early came to mean the *prescribed* manner; that which the recognised
authorities, patriarchal, judicial, or political, would enforce. *Recht*, from
which came *right* and *righteous*, is synonymous with law. The original
meaning indeed of *recht* did not point to law, but to physical straightness;
as *wrong* and its Latin equivalents meant twisted or *tortuous*; and from this
it is argued that right did not originally mean law, but on the contrary law
meant right. But however this may be, the fact that *recht* and *droit* became
restricted in their meaning to positive law, although much which is not
required by law is equally necessary to moral straightness or rectitude, is as
significant of the original character of moral ideas as if the derivation had
been the reverse way. The courts of justice, the administration of justice,
are the courts and the administration of law. *La justice*, in French, is the
established term for judicature. There can, I think, be no doubt that the
idée mère, the primitive element, in the formation of the notion of justice,
was conformity to law. It constituted the entire idea among the Hebrews,
up to the birth of Christianity; as might be expected in the case of a people
whose laws attempted to embrace all subjects on which precepts were
required, and who believed those laws to be a direct emanation from the
Supreme Being. But other nations, and in particular the Greeks and
Romans, who knew that their laws had been made originally, and still continued to be made, by men, were not afraid to admit that those men might
make bad laws; might do, by law, the same things, and from the same
motives, which, if done by individuals without the sanction of law, would
be called unjust. And hence the sentiment of injustice came to be attached,
not to all violations of law, but only to violations of such laws as *ought* to
exist, including such as ought to exist but do not; and to laws themselves, if
supposed to be contrary to what ought to be law. In this manner the idea of
law and of its injunctions was still predominant in the notion of justice,
even when the laws actually in force ceased to be accepted as the standard
of it.

13   It is true that mankind consider the idea of justice and its obligations as
applicable to many things which neither are, nor is it desired that they
should be, regulated by law. Nobody desires that laws should interfere
with the whole detail of private life; yet every one allows that in all daily
conduct a person may and does show himself to be either just or unjust.
But even here, the idea of the breach of what ought to be law, still lingers

in a modified shape. It would always give us pleasure, and chime in with our feelings of fitness, that acts which we deem unjust should be punished, though we do not always think it expedient that this should be done by the tribunals. We forego that gratification on account of incidental inconveni-   10
ences. We should be glad to see just conduct enforced and injustice repressed, even in the minutest details, if we were not, with reason, afraid of trusting the magistrate with so unlimited an amount of power over individuals. When we think that a person is bound in justice to do a thing, it is an ordinary form of language to say, that he ought to be compelled to   15
do it. We should be gratified to see the obligation enforced by anybody who had the power. If we see that its enforcement by law would be inexpedient, we lament the impossibility, we consider the impunity given to injustice as an evil, and strive to make amends for it by bringing a strong expression of our own and the public disapprobation to bear upon   20
the offender. Thus the idea of legal constraint is still the generating idea of the notion of justice, though undergoing several transformations before that notion, as it exists in an advanced state of society, becomes complete.

The above is, I think, a true account, as far as it goes, of the origin and   **14**
progressive growth of the idea of justice. But we must observe, that it con-
tains, as yet, nothing to distinguish that obligation from moral obligation in general. For the truth is, that the idea of penal sanction, which is the essence of law, enters not only into the conception of injustice, but into   5
that of any kind of wrong. We do not call anything wrong, unless we mean to imply that a person ought to be punished in some way or other for doing it; if not by law, by the opinion of his fellow creatures; if not by opinion, by the reproaches of his own conscience. This seems the real turning point of the distinction between morality and simple expediency.   10
It is a part of the notion of Duty in every one of its forms, that a person may rightfully be compelled to fulfil it. Duty is a thing which may be *exacted* from a person, as one exacts a debt. Unless we think that it might be exacted from him, we do not call it his duty. Reasons of prudence, or the interest of other people, may militate against actually exacting it; but the   15
person himself, it is clearly understood, would not be entitled to complain. There are other things, on the contrary, which we wish that people should do, which we like or admire them for doing, perhaps dislike or despise them for not doing, but yet admit that they are not bound to do; it is not a case of moral obligation; we do not blame them, that is, we do not think   20
that they are proper objects of punishment. How we come by these ideas of deserving and not deserving punishment, will appear, perhaps, in the

sequel; but I think there is no doubt that this distinction lies at the bottom of the notions of right and wrong; that we call any conduct wrong, or
25 employ, instead, some other term of dislike or disparagement, according as we think that the person ought, or ought not, to be punished for it; and we say that it would be right to do so and so, or merely that it would be desirable or laudable, according as we would wish to see the person whom it concerns, compelled, or only persuaded and exhorted, to act in that
30 manner.*

15 This, therefore, being the characteristic difference which marks off, not justice, but morality in general, from the remaining provinces of Expediency and Worthiness; the character is still to be sought which distinguishes justice from other branches of morality. Now it is known that
5 ethical writers divide moral duties into two classes, denoted by the ill-chosen expressions, duties of perfect and of imperfect obligation; the latter being those in which, though the act is obligatory, the particular occasions of performing it are left to our choice; as in the case of charity or beneficence, which we are indeed bound to practise, but not towards any
10 definite person, nor at any prescribed time. In the more precise language of philosophic jurists, duties of perfect obligation are those duties in virtue of which a correlative *right* resides in some person or persons; duties of imperfect obligation are those moral obligations which do not give birth to any right. I think it will be found that this distinction exactly coincides
15 with that which exists between justice and the other obligations of morality. In our survey of the various popular acceptations of justice, the term appeared generally to involve the idea of a personal right—a claim on the part of one or more individuals, like that which the law gives when it confers a proprietary or other legal right. Whether the injustice consists
20 in depriving a person of a possession, or in breaking faith with him, or in treating him worse than he deserves, or worse than other people who have no greater claims, in each case the supposition implies two things—a wrong done, and some assignable person who is wronged. Injustice may also be done by treating a person better than others; but the wrong in this
25 case is to his competitors, who are also assignable persons. It seems to me that this feature in the case—a right in some person, correlative to the moral obligation—constitutes the specific difference between justice, and generosity or beneficence. Justice implies something which it is not only right to do, and wrong not to do, but which some individual person can

* See this point enforced and illustrated by Professor Bain in an admirable chapter (entitled "The Ethical Emotions, or the Moral Sense"), of the second of the two treatises composing his elaborate and profound work on the Mind.

claim from us as his moral right. No one has a moral right to our generos- 30
ity or beneficence, because we are not morally bound to practise those
virtues towards any given individual. And it will be found with respect to
this as with respect to every correct definition, that the instances which
seem to conflict with it are those which most confirm it. For if a moralist
attempts, as some have done, to make out that mankind generally, though 35
not any given individual, have a right to all the good we can do them, he at
once, by that thesis, includes generosity and beneficence within the category of justice. He is obliged to say, that our utmost exertions are *due* to
our fellow creatures, thus assimilating them to a debt; or that nothing less
can be a sufficient *return* for what society does for us, thus classing the case 40
as one of gratitude; both of which are acknowledged cases of justice.
Wherever there is a right, the case is one of justice, and not of the virtue of
beneficence: and whoever does not place the distinction between justice
and morality in general where we have now placed it, will be found to
make no distinction between them at all, but to merge all morality in 45
justice.

Having thus endeavoured to determine the distinctive elements which 16
enter into the composition of the idea of justice, we are ready to enter on
the inquiry, whether the feeling, which accompanies the idea, is attached
to it by a special dispensation of nature, or whether it could have grown
up, by any known laws, out of the idea itself; and in particular, whether it 5
can have originated in considerations of general expediency.

I conceive that the sentiment itself does not arise from anything which 17
would commonly, or correctly, be termed an idea of expediency; but that
though, the sentiment does not, whatever is moral in it does.

We have seen that the two essential ingredients in the sentiment of 18
justice are, the desire to punish a person who has done harm, and the
knowledge or belief that there is some definite individual or individuals to
whom harm has been done.

Now it appears to me, that the desire to punish a person who has done 19
harm to some individual, is a spontaneous outgrowth from two sentiments, both in the highest degree natural, and which either are or
resemble instincts; the impulse of self-defence, and the feeling of
sympathy. 5

It is natural to resent, and to repel or retaliate, any harm done or 20
attempted against ourselves, or against those with whom we sympathize.
The origin of this sentiment it is not necessary here to discuss. Whether
it be an instinct or a result of intelligence, it is, we know, common to all
animal nature; for every animal tries to hurt those who have hurt, or who 5

it thinks are about to hurt, itself or its young. Human beings, on this point, only differ from other animals in two particulars. First, in being capable of sympathizing, not solely with their offspring, or, like some of the more noble animals, with some superior animal who is kind to them, but with
10 all human, and even with all sentient, beings. Secondly, in having a more developed intelligence, which gives a wider range to the whole of their sentiments, whether self-regarding or sympathetic. By virtue of his superior intelligence, even apart from his superior range of sympathy, a human being is capable of apprehending a community of interest
15 between himself and the human society of which he forms a part, such that any conduct which threatens the security of the society generally, is threatening to his own, and calls forth his instinct (if instinct it be) of self-defence. The same superiority of intelligence, joined to the power of sympathizing with human beings generally, enables him to attach himself to
20 the collective idea of his tribe, his country, or mankind, in such a manner that any act hurtful to them rouses his instinct of sympathy, and urges him to resistance.

21 The sentiment of justice, in that one of its elements which consists of the desire to punish, is thus, I conceive, the natural feeling of retaliation or vengeance, rendered by intellect and sympathy applicable to those injuries, that is, to those hurts, which wound us through, or in common
5 with, society at large. This sentiment, in itself, has nothing moral in it; what is moral is, the exclusive subordination of it to the social sympathies, so as to wait on and obey their call. For the natural feeling tends to make us resent indiscriminately whatever any one does that is disagreeable to us; but when moralized by the social feeling, it only acts in the directions
10 conformable to the general good: just persons resenting a hurt to society, though not otherwise a hurt to themselves, and not resenting a hurt to themselves, however painful, unless it be of the kind which society has a common interest with them in the repression of.

22 It is no objection against this doctrine to say, that when we feel our sentiment of justice outraged, we are not thinking of society at large, or of any collective interest, but only of the individual case. It is common enough certainly, though the reverse of commendable, to feel resentment
5 merely because we have suffered pain; but a person whose resentment is really a moral feeling, that is, who considers whether an act is blameable before he allows himself to resent it—such a person, though he may not say expressly to himself that he is standing up for the interest of society, certainly does feel that he is asserting a rule which is for the benefit of
10 others as well as for his own. If he is not feeling this—if he is regarding the

act solely as it affects him individually—he is not consciously just; he is not concerning himself about the justice of his actions. This is admitted even by anti-utilitarian moralists. When Kant (as before remarked) propounds as the fundamental principle of morals, 'So act, that thy rule of conduct might be adopted as a law by all rational beings,' he virtually acknow- 15 ledges that the interest of mankind collectively, or at least of mankind indiscriminately, must be in the mind of the agent when conscientiously deciding on the morality of the act. Otherwise he uses words without a meaning: for, that a rule even of utter selfishness could not *possibly* be adopted by all rational beings—that there is any insuperable obstacle in 20 the nature of things to its adoption—cannot be even plausibly maintained. To give any meaning to Kant's principle, the sense put upon it must be, that we ought to shape our conduct by a rule which all rational beings might adopt *with benefit to their collective interest.*

To recapitulate: the idea of justice supposes two things; a rule of 23 conduct, and a sentiment which sanctions the rule. The first must be sup- posed common to all mankind, and intended for their good. The other (the sentiment) is a desire that punishment may be suffered by those who infringe the rule. There is involved, in addition, the conception of some 5 definite person who suffers by the infringement; whose rights (to use the expression appropriated to the case) are violated by it. And the sentiment of justice appears to me to be, the animal desire to repel or retaliate a hurt or damage to oneself, or to those with whom one sympathizes, widened so as to include all persons, by the human capacity of enlarged sympathy, 10 and the human conception of intelligent self-interest. From the latter ele- ments, the feeling derives its morality; from the former, its peculiar impressiveness, and energy of self-assertion.

I have, throughout, treated the idea of a *right* residing in the injured 24 person, and violated by the injury, not as a separate element in the composition of the idea and sentiment, but as one of the forms in which the other two elements clothe themselves. These elements are, a hurt to some assignable person or persons on the one hand, and a demand for 5 punishment on the other. An examination of our own minds, I think, will show, that these two things include all that we mean when we speak of vio- lation of a right. When we call anything a person's right, we mean that he has a valid claim on society to protect him in the possession of it, either by the force of law, or by that of education and opinion. If he has what we 10 consider a sufficient claim, on whatever account, to have something guar- anteed to him by society, we say that he has a right to it. If we desire to prove that anything does not belong to him by right, we think this done as

soon as it is admitted that society ought not to take measures for securing
it to him, but should leave it to chance, or to his own exertions. Thus, a
person is said to have a right to what he can earn in fair professional competition; because society ought not to allow any other person to hinder
him from endeavouring to earn in that manner as much as he can. But he
has not a right to three hundred a-year, though he may happen to be
earning it; because society is not called on to provide that he shall earn that
sum. On the contrary, if he owns ten thousand pounds three per cent
stock, he *has* a right to three hundred a-year; because society has come
under an obligation to provide him with an income of that amount.

To have a right, then, is, I conceive, to have something which society
ought to defend me in the possession of. If the objector goes on to ask why
it ought, I can give him no other reason than general utility. If that expression does not seem to convey a sufficient feeling of the strength of the
obligation, nor to account for the peculiar energy of the feeling, it is
because there goes to the composition of the sentiment, not a rational
only but also an animal element, the thirst for retaliation; and this thirst
derives its intensity, as well as its moral justification, from the extraordin-
arily important and impressive kind of utility which is concerned. The
interest involved is that of security, to every one's feelings the most vital of
all interests. Nearly all other earthly benefits are needed by one person, not
needed by another; and many of them can, if necessary, be cheerfully fore-
gone, or replaced by something else; but security no human being can possibly do without; on it we depend for all our immunity from evil, and for
the whole value of all and every good, beyond the passing moment; since
nothing but the gratification of the instant could be of any worth to us,
if we could be deprived of everything the next instant by whoever was
momentarily stronger than ourselves. Now this most indispensable of all
necessaries, after physical nutriment, cannot be had, unless the machinery
for providing it is kept unintermittedly in active play. Our notion, therefore, of the claim we have on our fellow-creatures to join in making safe
for us the very groundwork of our existence, gathers feelings round it so
much more intense than those concerned in any of the more common
cases of utility, that the difference in degree (as is often the case in psychology) becomes a real difference in kind. The claim assumes that character
of absoluteness, that apparent infinity, and incommensurability with all
other considerations, which constitute the distinction between the feeling
of right and wrong and that of ordinary expediency and inexpediency. The
feelings concerned are so powerful, and we count so positively on finding
a responsive feeling in others (all being alike interested), that *ought* and

should grow into *must*, and recognised indispensability becomes a moral necessity, analogous to physical, and often not inferior to it in binding force.

If the preceding analysis, or something resembling it, be not the correct **26** account of the notion of justice; if justice be totally independent of utility, and be a standard *per se*, which the mind can recognise by simple introspection of itself; it is hard to understand why that internal oracle is so ambiguous, and why so many things appear either just or unjust, accord 5 ing to the light in which they are regarded.

We are continually informed that Utility is an uncertain standard, which **27** every different person interprets differently, and that there is no safety but in the immutable, ineffaceable, and unmistakeable dictates of Justice, which carry their evidence in themselves, and are independent of the fluctuations of opinion. One would suppose from this that on questions of 5 justice there could be no controversy; that if we take that for our rule, its application to any given case could leave us in as little doubt as a mathematical demonstration. So far is this from being the fact, that there is as much difference of opinion, and as fierce discussion, about what is just, as about what is useful to society. Not only have different nations and individ 10 uals different notions of justice, but, in the mind of one and the same individual, justice is not some one rule, principle, or maxim, but many, which do not always coincide in their dictates, and in choosing between which, he is guided either by some extraneous standard, or by his own personal predilections. 15

For instance, there are some who say, that it is unjust to punish anyone **28** for the sake of example to others; that punishment is just, only when intended for the good of the sufferer himself. Others maintain the extreme reverse, contending that to punish persons who have attained years of discretion, for their own benefit, is despotism and injustice, since if the 5 matter at issue is solely their own good, no one has a right to control their own judgment of it; but that they may justly be punished to prevent evil to others, this being an exercise of the legitimate right of self-defence. Mr Owen, again, affirms that it is unjust to punish at all; for the criminal did not make his own character; his education, and the circumstances which 10 surround him, have made him a criminal, and for these he is not responsible. All these opinions are extremely plausible; and so long as the question is argued as one of justice simply, without going down to the principles which lie under justice and are the source of its authority, I am unable to see how any of these reasoners can be refuted. For, in truth, 15 every one of the three builds upon rules of justice confessedly true. The

first appeals to the acknowledged injustice of singling out an individual, and making him a sacrifice, without his consent, for other people's benefit. The second relies on the acknowledged justice of self-defence, and the
20 admitted injustice of forcing one person to conform to another's notions of what constitutes his good. The Owenite invokes the admitted principle, that it is unjust to punish anyone for what he cannot help. Each is triumphant so long as he is not compelled to take into consideration any other maxims of justice than the one he has selected; but as soon as their
25 several maxims are brought face to face, each disputant seems to have exactly as much to say for himself as the others. No one of them can carry out his own notion of justice without trampling upon another equally binding. These are difficulties; they have always been felt to be such; and many devices have been invented to turn rather than to overcome them. As a
30 refuge from the last of the three, men imagined what they called the freedom of the will; fancying that they could not justify punishing a man whose will is in a thoroughly hateful state, unless it be supposed to have come into that state through no influence of anterior circumstances. To escape from the other difficulties, a favourite contrivance has been the
35 fiction of a contract, whereby at some unknown period all the members of society engaged to obey the laws, and consented to be punished for any disobedience to them; thereby giving to their legislators the right, which it is assumed they would not otherwise have had, of punishing them, either for their own good or for that of society. This happy thought was consid-
40 ered to get rid of the whole difficulty, and to legitimate the infliction of punishment, in virtue of another received maxim of justice, *volenti non fit injuria*; that is not unjust which is done with the consent of the person who is supposed to be hurt by it. I need hardly remark, that even if the consent were not a mere fiction, this maxim is not superior in authority to the
45 others which it is brought in to supersede. It is, on the contrary, an instructive specimen of the loose and irregular manner in which supposed principles of justice grow up. This particular one evidently came into use as a help to the coarse exigencies of courts of law, which are sometimes obliged to be content with very uncertain presumptions, on account of
50 the greater evils which would often arise from any attempt on their part to cut finer. But even courts of law are not able to adhere consistently to the maxim, for they allow voluntary engagements to be set aside on the ground of fraud, and sometimes on that of mere mistake or misinformation.

29   Again, when the legitimacy of inflicting punishment is admitted, how many conflicting conceptions of justice come to light in discussing the proper apportionment of punishment to offences. No rule on this subject recommends itself so strongly to the primitive and spontaneous sentiment of justice, as the *lex talionis*, an eye for an eye and a tooth for a tooth. Though this principle of the Jewish and of the Mahomedan law has been generally abandoned in Europe as a practical maxim, there is, I suspect, in most minds, a secret hankering after it; and when retribution accidentally falls on an offender in that precise shape, the general feeling of satisfaction evinced, bears witness how natural is the sentiment to which this repayment in kind is acceptable. With many the test of justice in penal infliction is that the punishment should be proportioned to the offence; meaning that it should be exactly measured by the moral guilt of the culprit (whatever be their standard for measuring moral guilt): the consideration, what amount of punishment is necessary to deter from the offence, having nothing to do with the question of justice, in their estimation: while there are others to whom that consideration is all in all; who maintain that it is not just, at least for man, to inflict on a fellow-creature, whatever may be his offences, any amount of suffering beyond the least that will suffice to prevent him from repeating, and others from imitating, his misconduct.

To take another example from a subject already once referred to. In a co-operative industrial association, is it just or not that talent or skill should give a title to superior remuneration? On the negative side of the question it is argued, that whoever does the best he can, deserves equally well, and ought not in justice to be put in a position of inferiority for no fault of his own; that superior abilities have already advantages more than enough, in the admiration they excite, the personal influence they command, and the internal sources of satisfaction attending them, without adding to these a superior share of the world's goods; and that society is bound in justice rather to make compensation to the less favoured, for this unmerited inequality of advantages, than to aggravate it. On the contrary side it is contended, that society receives more from the more efficient labourer; that his services being more useful, society owes him a larger return for them; that a greater share of the joint result is actually his work, and not to allow his claim to it is a kind of robbery; that if he is only to receive as much as others, he can only be justly required to produce as much, and to give a smaller amount of time and exertion, proportioned to his superior efficiency. Who shall decide between these appeals to conflicting principles of justice? Justice has in this case two sides to it, which it is impossible to bring into harmony, and the two disputants have chosen opposite sides; the one looks to what it is just that the individual should receive, the other to what it is just that the community should

give. Each, from his own point of view, is unanswerable; and any choice
between them, on grounds of justice, must be perfectly arbitrary. Social
25 utility alone can decide the preference.

31   How many, again, and how irreconcilable, are the standards of justice to
which reference is made in discussing the repartition of taxation. One
opinion is, that payment to the State should be in numerical proportion to
pecuniary means. Others think that justice dictates what they term gradu-
5 ated taxation; taking a higher percentage from those who have more to
spare. In point of natural justice a strong case might be made for disre-
garding means altogether, and taking the same absolute sum (whenever it
could be got) from every one: as the subscribers to a mess, or to a club, all
pay the same sum for the same privileges, whether they can all equally
10 afford it or not. Since the protection (it might be said) of law and government is afforded to, and is equally required by, all, there is no injustice in
making all buy it at the same price. It is reckoned justice, not injustice, that
a dealer should charge to all customers the same price for the same article,
not a price varying according to their means of payment. This doctrine, as
15 applied to taxation, finds no advocates, because it conflicts strongly with
men's feelings of humanity and perceptions of social expediency; but the
principle of justice which it invokes is as true and as binding as those which
can be appealed to against it. Accordingly, it exerts a tacit influence on the
line of defence employed for other modes of assessing taxation. People
20 feel obliged to argue that the State does more for the rich than for the poor,
as a justification for its taking more from them: though this is in reality not
true, for the rich would be far better able to protect themselves, in the
absence of law or government, than the poor, and indeed would probably
be successful in converting the poor into their slaves. Others, again, so far
25 defer to the same conception of justice, as to maintain that all should pay
an equal capitation tax for the protection of their persons (these being of
equal value to all), and an unequal tax for the protection of their property,
which is unequal. To this others reply, that the all of one man is as valuable
to him as the all of another. From these confusions there is no other mode
30 of extrication than the utilitarian.

32   Is, then, the difference between the Just and the Expedient a merely
imaginary distinction? Have mankind been under a delusion in thinking
that justice is a more sacred thing than policy, and that the latter ought only
to be listened to after the former has been satisfied? By no means. The
5 exposition we have given of the nature and origin of the sentiment, recog-
nises a real distinction; and no one of those who profess the most sublime

contempt for the consequences of actions as an element in their morality,
attaches more importance to the distinction than I do. While I dispute the
pretensions of any theory which sets up an imaginary standard of justice
not grounded on utility, I account the justice which is grounded on utility 10
to be the chief part, and incomparably the most sacred and binding part,
of all morality. Justice is a name for certain classes of moral rules, which
concern the essentials of human well-being more nearly, and are therefore
of more absolute obligation, than any other rules for the guidance of life;
and the notion which we have found to be of the essence of the idea of 15
justice, that of a right residing in an individual, implies and testifies to this
more binding obligation.

The moral rules which forbid mankind to hurt one another (in which **33**
we must never forget to include wrongful interference with each other's
freedom) are more vital to human well-being than any maxims, however
important, which only point out the best mode of managing some department of human affairs. They have also the peculiarity, that they are the 5
main element in determining the whole of the social feelings of mankind.
It is their observance which alone preserves peace among human beings:
if obedience to them were not the rule, and disobedience the exception,
every one would see in every one else a probable enemy, against whom he
must be perpetually guarding himself. What is hardly less important, these 10
are the precepts which mankind have the strongest and the most direct
inducements for impressing upon one another. By merely giving to each
other prudential instruction or exhortation, they may gain, or think they
gain, nothing: in inculcating on each other the duty of positive beneficence they have an unmistakeable interest, but far less in degree: a person 15
may possibly not need the benefits of others; but he always needs that they
should not do him hurt. Thus the moralities which protect every individual from being harmed by others, either directly or by being hindered in
his freedom of pursuing his own good, are at once those which he himself
has most at heart, and those which he has the strongest interest in publish- 20
ing and enforcing by word and deed. It is by a person's observance of these,
that his fitness to exist as one of the fellowship of human beings, is tested
and decided; for on that depends his being a nuisance or not to those with
whom he is in contact. Now it is these moralities primarily, which
compose the obligations of justice. The most marked cases of injustice, 25
and those which give the tone to the feeling of repugnance which charac-
terizes the sentiment; are acts of wrongful aggression, or wrongful exercise of power over some one; the next are those which consist in
wrongfully withholding from him something which is his due; in both

30 cases, inflicting on him a positive hurt, either in the form of direct suffering, or of the privation of some good which he had reasonable ground, either of a physical or of a social kind, for counting upon.

34 The same powerful motives which command the observance of these primary moralities, enjoin the punishment of those who violate them; and as the impulses of self-defence, of defence of others, and of vengeance, are all called forth against such persons, retribution, or evil for evil, becomes
5 closely connected with the sentiment of justice, and is universally included in the idea. Good for good is also one of the dictates of justice; and this, though its social utility is evident, and though it carries with it a natural human feeling, has not at first sight that obvious connexion with hurt or injury, which, existing in the most elementary cases of just and unjust, is
10 the source of the characteristic intensity of the sentiment. But the connexion, though less obvious, is not less real. He who accepts benefits, and denies a return of them when needed, inflicts a real hurt, by disappointing one of the most natural and reasonable of expectations, and one which he must at least tacitly have encouraged, otherwise the benefits would
15 seldom have been conferred. The important rank, among human evils and wrongs, of the disappointment of expectation, is shown in the fact that it constitutes the principal criminality of two such highly immoral acts as a breach of friendship and a breach of promise. Few hurts which human beings can sustain are greater, and none wound more, than when that on
20 which they habitually and with full assurance relied, fails them in the hour of need; and few wrongs are greater than this mere withholding of good; none excite more resentment, either in the person suffering, or in a sympathizing spectator. The principle, therefore, of giving to each what they deserve, that is, good for good as well as evil for evil, is not only included
25 within the idea of Justice as we have defined it, but is a proper object of that intensity of sentiment, which places the Just, in human estimation, above the simply Expedient.

35 Most of the maxims of justice current in the world, and commonly appealed to in its transactions, are simply instrumental to carrying into effect the principles of justice which we have now spoken of. That a person is only responsible for what he has done voluntarily, or could voluntarily
5 have avoided; that it is unjust to condemn any person unheard; that the punishment ought to be proportioned to the offence, and the like, are maxims intended to prevent the just principle of evil for evil from being perverted to the infliction of evil without that justification. The greater part of these common maxims have come into use from the practice
10 of courts of justice, which have been naturally led to a more complete

recognition and elaboration than was likely to suggest itself to others, of the rules necessary to enable them to fulfil their double function, of inflicting punishment when due, and of awarding to each person his right.

That first of judicial virtues, impartiality, is an obligation of justice, **36** partly for the reason last mentioned; as being a necessary condition of the fulfilment of the other obligations of justice. But this is not the only source of the exalted rank, among human obligations, of those maxims of equality and impartiality, which, both in popular estimation and in that of the 5 most enlightened, are included among the precepts of justice. In one point of view, they may be considered as corollaries from the principles already laid down. If it is a duty to do to each according to his deserts, returning good for good as well as repressing evil by evil, it necessarily follows that we should treat all equally well (when no higher duty forbids) who have 10 deserved equally well of us, and that society should treat all equally well who have deserved equally well of it, that is, who have deserved equally well absolutely. This is the highest abstract standard of social and distributive justice; towards which all institutions, and the efforts of all virtuous citizens, should be made in the utmost possible degree to converge. But 15 this great moral duty rests upon a still deeper foundation, being a direct emanation from the first principle of morals, and not a mere logical corollary from secondary or derivative doctrines. It is involved in the very meaning of Utility, or the Greatest-Happiness Principle. That principle is a mere form of words without rational signification, unless one person's 20 happiness, supposed equal in degree (with the proper allowance made for kind), is counted for exactly as much as another's. Those conditions being supplied, Bentham's dictum 'everybody to count for one, nobody for more than one,' might be written under the principle of utility as an explanatory commentary.* The equal claim of everybody to happiness in the 25

---

* This implication, in the first principle of the utilitarian scheme, of perfect impartiality between persons, is regarded by Mr Herbert Spencer (in his 'Social Statics') as a disproof of the pretensions of utility to be a sufficient guide to right; since (he says) the principle of utility presupposes the anterior principle, that everybody has an equal right to happiness. It may be more correctly described as supposing that equal amounts of happiness are equally desirable, whether felt by the same or by different persons. This, however, is not a presupposition; not a premise needful to support the principle of utility, but the very principle itself; for what is the principle of utility, if it be not that 'happiness' and 'desirable' are synonymous terms? If there is any anterior principle implied, it can be no other than this, that the truths of arithmetic are applicable to the valuation of happiness, as of all other measurable quantities.

[Mr Herbert Spencer, in a private communication on the subject of the preceding Note, objects to being considered an opponent of Utilitarianism, and states that he regards happiness as the ultimate end of morality; but deems that end only partially attainable by empirical

estimation of the moralist and the legislator, involves an equal claim to all the means of happiness, except in so far as the inevitable conditions of human life, and the general interest, in which that of every individual is included, set limits to the maxim; and those limits ought to be strictly con-
30 strued. As every other maxim of justice, so this, is by no means applied or held applicable universally; on the contrary, as I have already remarked, it bends to every person's ideas of social expediency. But in whatever case it is deemed applicable at all, it is held to be the dictate of justice. All persons are deemed to have a *right* to equality of treatment, except when some
35 recognised social expediency requires the reverse. And hence all social inequalities which have ceased to be considered expedient, assume the character not of simple inexpediency, but of injustice, and appear so tyrannical, that people are apt to wonder how they ever could have been tolerated; forgetful that they themselves perhaps tolerate other inequalities
40 under an equally mistaken notion of expediency, the correction of which would make that which they approve seem quite as monstrous as what they have at last learnt to condemn. The entire history of social improvement has been a series of transitions, by which one custom or institution after another, from being a supposed primary necessity of social existence,
45 has passed into the rank of an universally stigmatized injustice and tyranny. So it has been with the distinctions of slaves and freemen, nobles and serfs, patricians and plebeians; and so it will be, and in part already is, with the aristocracies of colour, race, and sex.

37 It appears from what has been said, that justice is a name for certain moral requirements, which, regarded collectively, stand higher in the scale of social utility, and are therefore of more paramount obligation, than any others; though particular cases may occur in which some other social duty
5 is so important, as to overrule any one of the general maxims of justice.

generalizations from the observed results of conduct, and completely attainable only by deducing, from the laws of life and the conditions of existence, what kinds of action necessarily tend to produce happiness and what kinds to produce unhappiness. With the exception of the word "necessarily," I have no dissent to express from this doctrine; and (omitting that word) I am not aware that any modern advocate of utilitarianism is of a different opinion. Bentham, certainly, to whom in the *Social Statics* Mr Spencer particularly referred, is, least of all writers, chargeable with unwillingness to deduce the effect of actions on happiness from the laws of human nature and the universal conditions of human life. The common charge against him is of relying too exclusively upon such deductions, and declining altogether to be bound by the generalizations from specific experience which Mr Spencer thinks that utilitarians generally confine themselves to. My own opinion (and, as I collect, Mr Spencer's) is, that in ethics, as in all other branches of scientific study, the consilience of the results of both these processes, each corroborating and verifying the other, is requisite to give to any general proposition the kind and degree of evidence which constitutes scientific proof.]

Thus, to save a life, it may not only be allowable, but a duty, to steal, or take by force, the necessary food or medicine, or to kidnap, and compel to officiate the only qualified medical practitioner. In such cases, as we do not call anything justice which is not a virtue, we usually say, not that justice must give way to some other moral principle, but that what is just in ordinary 10 cases is, by reason of that other principle, not just in the particular case. By this useful accommodation of language, the character of indefeasibility attributed to justice is kept up, and we are saved from the necessity of maintaining that there can be laudable injustice.

The considerations which have now been adduced resolve, I conceive, **38** the only real difficulty in the utilitarian theory of morals. It has always been evident that all cases of justice are also cases of expediency: the difference is in the peculiar sentiment which attaches to the former, as contradistinguished from the latter. If this characteristic sentiment has been 5 sufficiently accounted for; if there is no necessity to assume for it any peculiarity of origin; if it is simply the natural feeling of resentment, moralized by being made coextensive with the demands of social good; and if this feeling not only does but ought to exist in all the classes of cases to which the idea of justice corresponds; that idea no longer presents itself as a 10 stumbling-block to the utilitarian ethics. Justice remains the appropriate name for certain social utilities which are vastly more important, and therefore more absolute and imperative, than any others are as a class (though not more so than others may be in particular cases); and which, therefore, ought to be, as well as naturally are, guarded by a sentiment not 15 only different in degree, but also in kind; distinguished from the milder feeling which attaches to the mere idea of promoting human pleasure or convenience, at once by the more definite nature of its commands, and by the sterner character of its sanctions.

PART 3

Notes, Bibliography, and Index

Notes to *Utilitarianism*

CHAPTER 1. GENERAL REMARKS

Paragraph 1

4 **progress**: Mill believes that philosophical enquiry can enable us to approach an answer to the question of right and wrong. There can be moral knowledge; cf. *S* 8.943. On the continuing lack of consensus in ethics, cf. SD 10.64.

5 **the criterion of right and wrong**: i.e. the principle that states which properties of actions make them right or wrong.

6 **the dawn of philosophy**: Mill implies that philosophy began with the Greek philosophers before Socrates.

7 *summum bonum*: Latin, 'the highest good'. Mill links his own enquiry with that of the Greek philosophers, who offered accounts of *eudaimonia*, 'happiness', in terms of the 'good' for human beings (see e.g. Aristotle *c.*330 BC/1985: bk. 1). Some modern philosophers have sought to distinguish the question of 'the good' from that of 'the right'. For example, one might accept Mill's own account of what is good for human beings (pleasure), but deny his utilitarian moral theory.

foundation of morality: The morality Mill here has in mind is that set of principles by which we *should* act or live, not morality in the sense of *mores* or the particular moral beliefs instantiated in a culture.

14 **Socrates** (470–399 BC): teacher of Plato, condemned to death by the Athenian democracy for impiety and corrupting the young. He wrote nothing, but is the protagonist in Plato's dialogues.

Protagoras (490–420 BC): the most well known of the 'Sophists', a group of itinerant teachers. Famous for his relativistic doctrine that 'man is the measure of all things'. The dialogue referred to here is called *Protagoras* (Plato *c.*390 BC/1976). Mill first read it in the 'more advanced' period of his education after he had reached the age of 12 (*A* 1.21, 25).

15 **Plato** (428–347 BC): the most well-known ancient Greek philosopher. Mill says: 'There is no author to whom my father thought himself more indebted for his own mental culture, than Plato . . . I can bear similar testimony in regard to myself' (*A* 1.25).

16 **utilitarianism**: the doctrine that the right action is that which produces the greatest balance overall of pleasure over pain (see 2.2.1–5). Mill's interpretation of Socrates' position in the *Protagoras* could be questioned. First, the view that we should aim for the greatest balance of pleasure over pain may be expressed by Socrates only for ironic or argumentative purposes; it is certainly inconsistent with his position in other dialogues. Secondly, the hedonism of

the *Protagoras* is most plausibly seen as *egoistic* (i.e. as the view that one should seek to maximize *one's own* overall balance of pleasure over pain). Elsewhere, Mill accepts this interpretation, and recognizes hedonism as only one component of utilitarianism: G 11.391, 418; Letter to Grote (1862) 15.764. Mill sees utilitarianism as a broad church, and is keen to recruit members. For example, he speaks of 'the judicious utilitarianism of Aristotle' (*L* 18.235).

Paragraph 2

Mill draws a sharp contrast between sciences and 'arts' at the end of *A System of Logic*: 'Whatever speaks in rules, or precepts, not in assertions respecting matters of fact, is art; and ethics or morality, is properly a portion of the art corresponding to the sciences of human nature and society' (*S* 8.943). Here he notes that there is much dispute concerning the first principles even of mathematics, but that this does not mean that we should doubt that e.g. $2 + 2 = 4$. There is complete agreement on such matters, and the disagreement enters at a higher level (*Why* does $2 + 2 = 4$? How do we *know*?). Morality, however, is concerned with rules, and, Mill believes, rules must be directed towards an end or goal. This goal will be captured in the first principle of morality.

One of Mill's 'intuitionist' opponents might argue that there is a stronger analogy between mathematics and morality than Mill allows, since there is almost as much consensus on most moral issues as there is on basic arithmetic (Mill himself believes that we should accept *most* of customary morality). Also, it could be suggested, these rules need not be seen as having any point external to themselves, so that there is no need for a first principle independent of them. Just as $2 + 2 = 4$, so you should not, for example, torture an innocent child for fun.

12 **as full of fictions as English law**: cf. Bentham (1776 / 1977: 411): 'the pestilential breath of Fiction poisons the sense of every instrument it comes near. . . . The consequence is, that the Law . . . *still* wants much of being generally intelligible.'

20 **All action is for the sake of some end**: This is reminiscent of the opening sentence of Aristotle's *Nicomachean Ethics*.

Paragraph 3

Mill here sets up his debate as one between two 'schools' of philosophical thought: his opponents, the *intuitionists*, and the *inductivists*, among whom he counted himself. The intuitionists claimed that certain moral principles were self-evident, while Mill believed that these views could be explained in accordance with *empiricism* and *associationism* (empiricism is the view that all our knowledge is based on the evidence of our senses, while associationism states that mental events can be explained in terms of the laws governing the relations between these events; cf. *A* 1.269–70). His objections to intuitionism in this paragraph are: (i) there is no 'moral sense'; (ii) intuitionists often fail to offer foundational principles, assuming that common-sense moral views are enough on their own; (iii) they fail even more often to offer a single foundational principle to resolve conflicts between moral principles; and (iv) those they do offer are implausible. What is particularly interesting here is the link Mill draws between inductivism and utilitarianism. Strictly, there is nothing to stop an intuitionist advocating a utilitarian first principle, thus dealing with Mill's last three objections (see e.g. Sidgwick 1907: bk. 3, ch. 13). The intuitionist might then deal with the first objection by asserting that any form of understanding through the senses must be governed by some background principles which do not themselves arise through the senses, and that the same kind of principle can be found in ethics. It can be argued that a utilitarian, since the utilitarian principle itself is not discerned by the senses, is committed to some form of moral sense theory or intuitionism; see Spencer (1851: 22–3).

11 **the intuitive . . . school**: Mill's greatest intuitionist opponent was William Whewell (1794–1866). Mill criticizes him in the 'Essay on Whewell', written shortly before *Utilitarianism* (10.165–201). In Whewell (1837), conscience is said to be a truth-seeking faculty, the deliverances of which are indications of God's will (16–22; cf. Whewell 1845: vol. 1, 234–5; vol. 2, 6). On moral sense theories and the intuitive/inductive distinction, see *AC* 10.300–1; SD 10.51, 59–60. Mill saw intuitionists as conservative obstacles to moral progress, because of their sanctifying the customary morality of their day; cf. SD 10.73–4; W 168–9, 200.

18 **evident *à priori***: i.e. obviously correct, independently of further evidence.

21 **questions of observation and experience**: Mill's attempt to ground ethics on the observation of human psychology is in ch. 4.

33 **a determinate order of precedence**: on the need for a first principle, cf. *S* 8.951. Mill does not stop to consider the view that there may be several irreducible moral principles (e.g. 'Do not murder', 'Do not lie', 'Be kind to others'), the question of which applies in any situation being left to judgement rather than philosophy. This is probably because he would have equated such a view with a moral sense theory.

Paragraph 4

7 **tacit influence**: cf. Bentham (1789/1996: ch. 1, sect. 12).

12 **principle of utility**: i.e. utilitarianism; usually seen as a 'first principle', according to which the right action is that which maximizes the balance of happiness. Here Mill is speaking of it as one principle among others. There is, however, a great difference between the two understandings of the principle, since many of the objections to utilitarianism as a single principle consist in reference to values, such as integrity or justice, which it does not include.

Bentham (Jeremy Bentham 1748–1832): the first philosopher to count clearly as utilitarian, and a huge influence on Mill from Mill's earliest years. It was while reading Dumont's French edition of Bentham—the *Traités de législation*—in 1821 that Mill was 'converted' permanently to utilitarianism (*A* 1.67–71, 145). Any serious student of *Utilitarianism* should read Bentham's most famous work, *Introduction to the Principles of Morals and Legislation*.

12 **greatest happiness principle**: See R 10.5; first fn. in Bentham (1789/1996).

23 **Kant** (Immanuel Kant 1724–1804): German philosopher; the most influential anti-utilitarian moral philosopher. Mill is here referring to Kant's *Foundations of the Metaphysics of Morals* (1785). In that work Kant seeks to base ethics on rationality, with his famous 'Categorical Imperative', the essence of which is captured here in Mill's formulation (cf. Kant (1785/1995: 38 (421): the bracketed numbers in the references to Kant are to vol. 4 of the standard edition published by the Royal Prussian Academy of Sciences). Mill's objection is not entirely fair, since some of Kant's examples are of cases of laws that cannot be willed. I cannot will a world in which all beings make false promises when it is in their interest, since in such a world promising would not exist. But Mill is correct to point out that the content of what is rational or reasonable in Kant is often informed by reflection on the consequences of adopting certain laws.

Paragraph 5

5 **ultimate ends**: i.e. non-instrumental goods. Music can be shown to be a *means* to pleasure; but pleasure is an end in itself, and so cannot be proven in the same sense to be good; cf. 4.1.1–4.

6 **not amenable to direct proof**: cf. Bentham (1789/1996: 1.11).

12 **including all things which are in themselves good**: cf. 4.5–8; Aristotle (*c*.330 BC/1985: 1094^b14–20).

20 **intuition**: Note the contrast drawn here between intuition and the intellect's being swayed by considerations for or against some proposition. Mill's main objection to intuitionism is that it asserts certain things as good or bad, right or wrong, without argument. The intuitionist might respond that, at the end of an argument, the intellect can decide only by judging, and that this is the same as 'intuiting'.

Paragraph 6

1 **We shall examine**: See ch. 4.

11 **I shall offer some illustrations**: See chs. 2 and 3.

CHAPTER 2. WHAT UTILITARIANISM IS

Paragraph 1

4 **utility**: Mill is here referring to the use of 'utilitarian' as applied to, e.g. an ugly but cheap piece of furniture, designed for use rather than beauty. In the

utilitarian tradition, 'utility' sometimes meant, especially in economic writings, the properties of some object *instrumental* to pleasure. A glass of wine might have utility, in that it brings me pleasure. Here Mill equates utility with pleasure itself. He himself used the term in both senses; see e.g. *P* 2.46.

10 **an able writer**: I have been unable to identify this passage or its author.

14 **Epicurus**: ancient Athenian hedonist philosopher (342–270 BC). The word 'epicurean' has taken on the meaning 'devoted to sensual pleasures' because of the misrepresentation of later Greek writers, not because of the life or writings of Epicurus. Like Mill in this chapter, Epicurus explicitly claimed the superiority of mental over bodily pleasures. Epicurus' view can be seen as egoistic; see n. on 1.1.16. Mill recognized this; see *D* 27.666.

16 **pleasure itself, together with exemption from pain**: Mill does not point out sufficiently clearly that mere exemption from pain is not itself a good (cf. 2.2.4–5). On his view, pleasure is the only good, pain is the only bad, and the best action is that which brings about the greatest *balance* of pleasure over pain.

24 **pleasure in some of its forms**: Mill must mean the pleasure of contemplating beauty or ornament.

30 **discontinued it as a distinctive appellation**: After his breakdown at the age of 20, Mill began to dislike philosophical sectarianism, preferring, in Aristotelian fashion, to look for the truth in all views. See *A* 1.147.

33 *Annals of the Parish* (fn.): John Galt's novel was published in Edinburgh in 1821. The reference Mill makes is to a disparaging use of the term 'utilitarian' on p. 286. The *Autobiography* suggests that it was Mill's founding of the Utilitarian Society in 1822–3 that popularized the term (*A* 1.81).

utility as a standard (fn.): *Fraser's*: 'the standard'. In fact utilitarianism is almost always taken to be the view that utility is *the* standard; see n. on 1.4.12.

Paragraph 2

1 **the foundation of morals**: For another statement of utilitarianism, see B 10.III.

2 **actions are right**: 'Good' or 'bad' might have made better sense here, since the notion of one action's being 'more right' than another is a little odd. But Mill wishes utilitarianism to be a properly *moral* theory, and his meaning here is anyway clear enough. If an action produces happiness, it is—to that extent (see below)—right, and if it produces unhappiness it is to that extent wrong. *The* right action will be that which produces the greatest balance of happiness over unhappiness overall, the idea of maximization being implicit in the 'greatest' of the 'greatest happiness principle'. Mill elsewhere called the greatest happiness of the greatest number 'the only true end of morality' (BH 6.4). The question arises what one should do when morality conflicts with other spheres of practical reason, such as self-interest (or 'departments of the Art of Life': see *S* 8.949). Conflicts are to be decided by the utilitarian principle,

understood now as a supra-moral principle; see *S* 8.951. So, practically speaking, utilitarian morality is overriding. See Crisp (1997: 119–23).

3 **tend**: a technical word in the utilitarian tradition; see e.g. Bentham (1789/1996: 1.2). The tendency of an action to promote happiness is merely the extent to which that action promotes happiness.

4 **pleasure, and the absence of pain**: Mill is not as precise here as he might be, though his meaning is clear. Pleasure is good, whereas the absence of pain is not, being merely neutral. Below Mill speaks of the 'prevention' of pain. What he has in mind here is that removing or preventing suffering can be valuable: producing three units of pleasure, to put it crudely, is equivalent to preventing three units of pain. Mill discusses the nature of pleasure, and whether it is a sensation or a quality of a sensation, in *AP* 31.214.

6 **much more requires to be said**: See the rest of ch. 2.

9 **the theory of life**: This is Mill's hedonism: pleasurable or enjoyable experiences are the only good things, and they are good solely because of their pleasurableness or enjoyableness. Mill allowed his hedonism to guide his thought throughout his writings, including his economics and politics; see e.g. *O* 4.284, according to which all labour and expenditure are directed to enjoyment.

11 **(which are as numerous in the utilitarian as in any other scheme)**: cf. 4.4–8.

Paragraph 3

6 **followers of Epicurus**: The misrepresentation of Epicurus is described in Diogenes Laertius (*c*. 230/1958: bk. 10, chs. 3–12).

Paragraph 4

12 **do not regard anything as happiness which does not include their gratification**: This is not to be taken to mean that there is no happiness in the lives of animals. The use of 'happiness' Mill has in mind here is that in which one says, 'She had a happy life'. In this sense, one's life can be unhappy, and yet contain a certain amount of happiness. For another example of this use, see 2.12.18.

16 **Stoic, as well as Christian elements**: See 2.12, 16, 18, 22.

20 **utilitarian writers in general**: e.g. Bentham (1789/1996: ch. 4).

29 **quality . . . quantity**: 'Quantity' refers to the intensity and duration of the pleasurableness of an experience; cf. Bentham (1789/1996: 4.2). So, taking what Mill describes as the usual utilitarian line, one might claim that the pleasure of reading a poem is more valuable than that of drinking a lemonade because the poetic pleasure is more intense and stays with one longer. But one could also argue, as does Mill, that the very *nature* of the experience of reading poetry makes it more valuable. In the *Autobiography*, he suggests that his father had always rated 'intellectual enjoyments above all others, even in value as pleasures, independently of their ulterior benefits' (*A* 1.51). The quality/quan-

tity distinction, along with the pig and Socrates example, occur in Mill's diary of 1854: 27.663. Cf. *L* 18.224: 'I regard utility as the ultimate appeal on all ethical questions; but it must be utility in the largest sense, grounded on the permanent interests of man as a progressive being.'

Paragraph 5

1 **what I mean by difference of quality in pleasures**: Rather than say more about what he does mean, Mill goes on to discuss how one can determine which of two pleasures is the higher. His argument here is influenced by that in Plato (*c*.380 BC/1992: 581c–583a), where the philosopher is said to have the correct view of the various kinds of life available since he has experience of each.

4 **all or almost all**: So when competent judges disagree, the only solution is to accept the verdict of the majority.

5 **irrespective of any feeling of moral obligation**: So a preference for poetry over drinking based on a belief in, say, a moral duty to fulfil one's talents would not count.

Paragraph 6

3 **the manner of existence**: Note that preferring a life containing mental pleasures to a life without such pleasures is different from the preference of a mental pleasure to any amount of bodily pleasure discussed in para. 5.

15 **requires more to make him happy**: See n. on 2.4.12.

26 **sense of dignity**: cf. B 10.95–6.

28 **essential a part of happiness**: Mill's hedonism (see 2.2.4–5) suggests that he means here the pleasure of contemplating and acting upon one's sense of dignity.

Paragraph 7

4 **Men often . . . make their election for the nearer good**: This is what would ordinarily be called 'weakness of will'; but in Mill's terminology it is the *result* of will, understood as a habit which has detached itself from desire; see 4.11.

27 **though many, in all ages, have broken down in an ineffectual attempt to combine both**: This is an odd concession from Mill, since it seems that he is allowing that someone who is experienced in both kinds of pleasure may prefer a higher-lower combination to pure higher pleasure. Perhaps such preference should be put down to the 'infirmity of character' mentioned earlier.

Paragraph 8

2 **the best worth having of two pleasures**: See n. on 2.6.3.

Paragraph 9

10 **nobleness of character**: Mill probably has in mind here particularly the pleasures of the moral sentiments. The pleasures of the intellect and of the feelings
can be indulged in with an utter lack of concern for others; cf. *S* 8.952.

Paragraph 10

10 **the end of human action**: cf. n. on 2.2.2.
14 **the whole sentient creation**: Like Bentham, Mill includes sentient non-
human animals within the scope of morality; cf. *W* 10.185–7. The phrase 'so far
as the nature of things admits' perhaps illustrates Mill's recognition of the fact
that, since non-humans cannot experience higher pleasures, their contribution to the overall sum of happiness can only be small.

Paragraph 11

4 **What right hast thou to be happy?**: How Mill saw the relation of this question and that which follows it to the unattainability objection is not clear.
Certainly it is not equivalent to it, but it does not receive independent discussion in the text below. It is a weak objection, since it is quite consistent to claim
both that happiness is the rational purpose of human life and that no one has
a right to it or life as one of its conditions.
Mr Carlyle (Thomas Carlyle 1795–1881): Scottish radical social critic. Mill was
heavily influenced by Carlyle's romanticism, but their relationship suffered as
Carlyle began to realize that Mill did not see himself as a disciple of Carlyle.
The reference here is to Carlyle (1836: 193). *Utilitarianism* can be seen as a
response to the criticisms of the doctrine by Carlyle and others.
6 **Next, they say, that men can do *without* happiness**: This objection is inconsistent with the first. If happiness is unattainable, then one cannot renounce it.
8 **Entsagen**: German. The idea here is that morality must hurt if it is to be
truly virtuous; cf. Carlyle (1836: 193; 1840: 208–9).

Paragraph 12

5 **the prevention . . . of unhappiness**: As Mill implies, so-called 'negative utilitarianism' implies that we should destroy all sentient life, as painlessly as possible, so as to minimize unhappiness.
10 **Novalis**: pseudonym of Friedrich Leopold Freiherr von Hardenberg, an early
German romantic (1722–1801). Mill may well have become acquainted with his
work through Carlyle's review of Novalis's *Collected Works* in *Foreign Review*
(1829), 7 (repr. in Carlyle 1840: vol. 2, 191–261).
21 **active . . . passive**: Active pleasures involve physical or mental exercise (e.g.
running or constructing an argument), while passive pleasures include

'organic' pleasures, such as that of a full stomach, or emotional pleasures, such as love. See *E* 9.431; cf. *C* 19.406–12 (on the importance of political participation); *L* 18.260–75 (on individuality and the active character). Mill is again influenced here by Aristotle; see e.g. Aristotle (*c.*330 BC / 1985: 1098^{b}31–1099^{a}7).

Paragraph 13

5 **tranquillity, and excitement**: Tranquillity suggests freedom from pain, so little pleasure is required for a positive balance; excitement increases the intensity of pleasure, so that pain can be counterbalanced.

22 **especially those who have cultivated a fellow feeling with the collective interests of mankind**: On the role of the moral sentiments in happiness, see 2.4; 3.10; 4.5–8.

26 **mental cultivation**: Intellectual pleasures are higher; see 2.4.18.

Paragraph 14

The argument in this chapter that intellectual cultivation and virtue play central roles in happiness has ancient roots. See e.g. Aristotle (*c.*330 BC / 1985: bk. 1, ch. 7; bk. 10, ch. 7). The role of fortune in happiness, also discussed here, was another ancient theme; see e.g. Aristotle (*c.*330 BC / 1985: bk. 1, chs. 9–11).

24 **if human affairs continue to improve**: as Mill thought they would. He believed that the general tendency of humanity will be to progress 'towards a better and happier state' (*S* 8.913–14). This belief in progress was characteristic of much nineteenth-century thought.

34 **deprive us of those in whom our happiness is wrapt up**: Mill probably has in mind Harriet Taylor, who had died from 'pulmonary congestion' in 1858 (*A* 1.249).

Paragraph 15

In this paragraph, Mill argues that virtuous self-sacrifice is not a good thing in itself, independent of happiness. Cf. 4.5–8, where he argues that virtue can also be a part of happiness; and *TG* 11.149.

10 **this self-sacrifice must be for some end**: On the assumption that all action must be for some end, cf. 1.2.20 and n.

21 **the ascetic mounted on his pillar**: Mill has in mind St Simeon Stylites (390–459), who lived on pillars, the highest of which was twenty metres, for nearly forty years; see Farmer (1992: 436–7).

Paragraph 16

The argument of this paragraph again has ancient roots. Epicurus (see 2.1.14 and n.) believed that *ataraxia*, freedom from anxiety or tranquillity, was central to happiness. This view is also found in the Stoics; see Long and Sedley (1987: 113–14, 396).

12 **many a Stoic**: The Stoic school was founded in Athens in *c*.300 BC. Stoics believed that everything happens by divine providence, so one should accept with equanimity things which appear distressing. In the Roman period, the Stoics opposed some of the more dictatorial emperors, often suffering banishment or death as a consequence.

Paragraph 17

3 **Transcendentalist**: i.e. the Intuitionist, who believes in truths the evidence for which 'transcends' sense-experience. Mill has in mind particularly those who accept the 'transcendental' arguments of Kant.

Paragraph 18

5 **disinterested and benevolent spectator**: The idea of spelling out the moral point of view in terms of the point of view of a spectator was first fully developed by the Scottish philosopher Adam Smith (1723–90); see Smith (1759/1976: 82–5 and *passim*). Smith was influenced by the Stoics, and by David Hume (1711–76) and Francis Hutcheson (1694–1746/7).

6 **golden rule**: Some interpretations of the golden rule are problematic. For example, if I am a masochist, it might appear that the golden rule requires me to inflict pain upon you. Mill assumes that each person desires his own happiness, and that loving one's neighbours as oneself will lead one to be entirely impartial between their happiness and one's own. This interpretation of the golden rule is radical, since it was not usually understood to require complete impartiality in this sense.

10 **laws and social arrangements . . . education and opinion**: Mill's discussion of moral education here is probably influenced by Aristotle (*c*.330 BC/1985: bk. 10, ch. 9). On the harmony of self-interest and concern for others, see 3.10; and cf. Aristotle (*c*.330 BC/1985: bk. 9, ch. 8).

15 **association**: According to the theory of association, education might establish associations between pleasure and acting morally.

21 **one of the habitual motives of action**: So reference to, and motivation by, the utilitarian principle will play a part in human decision-making and action, alongside other motives.

28 **springs of action**: cf. *A Table of the Springs of Action* in Bentham 1983; also Bentham (1789/1996: ch. 10).

Paragraph 19

This paragraph, and the footnote to it added by Mill in the 2nd edn., are among the most complex passages in *Utilitarianism*. The distinction between what moti-

vates the moral agent and the deliverances of ethical theory predates Mill. See
e.g. Butler (1726/1897: vol. 2, sermon 2, sects. 7, 10), where Butler suggests that virtuous parents will show natural affection for their children, and that the task of
conscience is to decide, by reflection, which natural affections to follow. Cf. James
Mill (1835: 158).

1 **The objectors to utilitarianism . . . under greater obligations**:   The objector suggests that utilitarianism's demand that people act so as to promote the
greatest overall happiness, rather than their own happiness or that of those
close to them, is excessive. This could mean either that human beings cannot
act on such a motive, or that they cannot reasonably be expected to. Mill
distinguishes between the utilitarian standard—the principle that utility
should be maximized—and the actual motives of agents. Utilitarianism
does not require agents always to be attempting to follow it (see Introd.,
Sect. 6).

   Mill says that it is particularly unfair so to criticize utilitarianism, since utilitarians have insisted that motives have nothing to do with the morality of
actions (cf. PL 1.323). What matters to utilitarians is the greatest balance of
pleasure over pain, not how it comes about. If someone saves a person from
drowning, thus maximizing utility, it does not matter *why* they did it.

21 **An opponent . . . hurtful actions are likely to arise** (fn.):   John Llewelyn (*sic*)
Davies (1826–1916), a theologian and political liberal, objects to Mill's claim
that motives are morally irrelevant, introducing the example of the tyrant
who saves the man from drowning so as to torture him. Mill's response is com-
pressed and hard to interpret. We might expect him to draw attention to the
difference between the consequences in the tyrant case and those in his examples. What he in fact says is that, because the intention is different, this is a
different act.

   Mill's claim, here, rests on his view that an action has two components: an
intention, and its effects (*S* 7.55). So if you change the intention, you change
the action. Intention consists in the foresight of consequences (*AP* 31.253), and
the tyrant foresees overall bad consequences, while in Mill's original rescue
cases, the agents would—we assume—have foreseen overall good consequences. In the tyrant case, Mill would perhaps have suggested that we ought
to construe the action as one of, say, 'persecution', the 'first step' of which
involves fishing the man out of the sea. It is, however, as Mill himself admits,
still a rescue. He may be assuming that, when assessing the morality of an
action, one should employ that description of it which best brings out both its
pleasurable and painful consequences for those involved and the agent's
beliefs about those consequences (on the possibility of alternative descrip-
tions, cf. Bentham 1789/1996: 7.20).

   Mill distinguishes intentions from motives, claiming that 'the morality of
the action depends entirely upon the intention—that is, upon what the agent
wills to do' (cf. James Mill 1835: 161–4). As it stands, this is inconsistent with

Mill's utilitarianism as stated in 2.2, according to which the morality of an action depends entirely upon the pleasure and pain it produces.

Mill refers here to Bentham. Like Mill, Bentham believes that the morality of an action depends upon its pleasurable and painful consequences (1789/1996: 7.1–3). Strictly speaking, both motives and intentions are morally irrelevant (ibid. 8.13). What does Bentham mean by motives? A motive is something that influences the will, an idea of pleasure or pain. And, since only pleasures and pains are good and bad respectively, motives cannot be good or bad in themselves (ibid. 10.9–10). Nor can one claim that certain motives are good or bad because they tend generally to lead to good or bad consequences, since any motive can produce any result (ibid. 10.12).

Intentions can be distinguished from motives (ibid. 9.15). Imagine that, out of malice, you prosecute me for a crime of which I am innocent. The consequences of your action will primarily be the effect upon me, and that will be bad. Your motive is malice, and this will be called bad. But the consequences *would* have been good if they had been such as you believed them to be (the punishment of a criminal who might otherwise commit his crime again). Your intention involves 'consciousness' (which is in this case false) of the consequences your proposed action will bring about, and an intention can be said to be good if those assumed consequences are good, bad if they are bad (ibid. 8.13). In the tyrant case, the consequences of which the tyrant is 'conscious' are bad, so the intention could be said to be bad.

Mill almost certainly had something like this view in mind in writing this note. In the *AP* passage referred to above, he claims that intention constitutes the rightness or wrongness of the act. So if the agent foresees overall bad consequences, he is guilty, and if overall good, praiseworthy. To attain consistency with utilitarianism, in both Mill's and Bentham's case, these claims about intention are best interpreted as advice about when to blame and praise agents, rather than as attempts to offer a 'standard of morals' (cf. *B* 10.112). It may be that the best way to understand Mill's 'entirely' here is as follows: in so far as the morality of an action depends either on intention or on motive, it depends entirely upon intention.

Mill says that a motive is morally irrelevant 'when it ['if it' until the 4th edn.] makes no difference in the act'. This implies that a motive *can* make a difference when it does make a difference in the act. Bentham allows that this can occur, so that individual motives can be said to be good or bad in particular cases (1789/1996: 10.33). But Davies's objection concerns just such a case, so it begins to appear that Mill should have accepted his point. For if Mill is willing to allow that the morality of an action can depend on its intention, because of its influence on consequences, he should accept that a motive such as that of the tyrant in Davies's example can also be said to be morally relevant. What should then play the main role in the response to Davies would be, as I suggested above, the claim that what matter ultimately to utilitarians are the pleasures and pains produced by actions, not, directly, either the intentions that lead to the actions, or the motives that lead to the intentions.

It is worth noting, finally, that, though Mill allows that motives are relevant to our estimation of the agent himself, he again puts stress on the dispositions of the agent to perform 'useful, or . . . hurtful actions'. For Bentham, the effects on actions would have been all that counted. One should not criticize a disposition except in so far as it is likely to do harm, nor praise it in so far as it is likely to do good. Again, Mill's implication here that moral praise and blame may be justified in other contexts does not sit easily with his utilitarianism. It is, however, an implication he denies in the penultimate sentence of 2.20.

21 **But to speak only of actions done . . . habitually about so large an object**: After the fn., Mill moves to consider those few cases in which utilitarianism *does* require action from a sense of duty, and claims that the theory does not demand that we act with the whole world, or even society, in mind. Rather, we should in most circumstances concern ourselves only with the happiness of those most directly involved with our actions, except to the extent that we must be sure that our actions are not violating anyone's rights. Mill's utilitarian account of rights is defended in ch. 5, the argument essentially being that a society in which rights are respected will be happier than one in which they are not (see esp. 5.25).

Mill's stated reason for the limited range of moral concern is that very few people have the chance to be benefactors on an extended scale (cf. SD 10.59). This argument is dubious. Because utilitarians are concerned with the outcome of our actions, and not just their immediate causal upshot, acting in such a way e.g. that many people will suffer and die as a consequence will usually be unjustifiable. But Mill is advocating that his readers continue to act in this way, thinking only about the interests of those close to them, and ignoring the plight of those whose suffering and death they might prevent, for example by donating money to or working for a charity.

There are other, stronger arguments for the limitation of concern which are analogous to the argument for rights. Because human beings have limited motivational resources, it may be better *in terms of overall happiness* if they concern themselves, and are encouraged to concern themselves, primarily only with that subset of sentient beings whose interests they can be moved to act to promote. Encouraging impartial altruism could be self-defeating, sapping partial concern while failing to provide any less partial alternative. Nevertheless, it is unlikely that encouraging some degree of impartial concern greater than the norm would be anything other than highly beneficial. Mill was quite aware of this argument, and would have accepted its gist. In *Auguste Comte and Positivism* he says that duty should not be exaggerated, and that there is a region between duty and sin, known as worthiness: 'It is not good that persons should be bound, by other people's opinion, to do everything that they would deserve praise for doing. There is a standard of altruism to which all should be required to come up, and a degree beyond which it is not obligatory, but meritorious' (10.337). ('Worthiness' here refers to super-erogation and is not necessarily confined to the 'Aesthetic' department of the Art of Life; see *S* 8.949; and n. on 2.2.2.) Mill goes on to say that in an improving society, the domain of duty is always widening. Cf. 2.21.6 and n., 5.14.10 and n.

26 **of which the good of the world is made up**: Mill is an individualist, in the sense that the good of society or any group consists only in the goods instantiated in the lives of its members; cf. 4.3.8.

39 **In the case of abstinences indeed . . . pernicious to society**: The last two sentences of this paragraph constitute another crux of Millian interpretation. Some have understood this passage to be advocating a version of *indirect utilitarianism*, sometimes called *utilitarian generalization*, according to which an action is wrong if it is in a class which, if performed generally, would fail to maximize utility (see Introd., Sect. 5). This view would be logically inconsistent with Mill's apparent commitment to *act utilitarianism*, according to which the right act is the one that produces the greatest balance of pleasure over pain (2.2). It would also be inconsistent in practice, since act utilitarianism might speak in favour of a maximizing act even though it was in a non-maximizing class of acts. (See Letter to H. S. Brandreth (1867) 16.1234.)

It must be admitted that Mill is not always entirely clear about the distinction between various forms of utilitarianism (see e.g. R 10.7). This present passage can, however, be understood in line with act utilitarianism. First, in speaking of 'obligation' here, Mill almost certainly means 'sense of obligation', our having this sense being something justifiable by the utility principle. Secondly, Mill does not say that the consequences in the case he is imagining *are* beneficial (i.e. utility-maximizing), only that they *might* be. So Mill is thinking of a situation in which an agent sees that customary morality requires him, say, not to lie, but also that going against customary morality might be beneficial overall. Mill suggests that they should respect their sense of obligation. Why? Because of the benefits of the general acceptance of customary moral rules; see 2.23–4; *AP* 31.253; *S* 8.1154–5; *W* 181–3.

It should also be noted that Mill believed that often the best way of working out the consequences of a particular act was to consider the consequences of the class of acts to which it belonged; see Letter to J. Venn (1872) 17.1881–2.

Paragraph 20

1 **The same considerations**: i.e. the distinction between the standard of morality and the motives of agents.

4 **It is often affirmed**: Consider e.g. the character of Gradgrind in Charles Dickens's *Hard Times* (1854).

8 **If the assertion means**: Mill is here slightly disingenuous. The obvious interpretation of the objection is the one he considers in the following paragraph.

14 **These considerations are relevant, not to the estimation of actions, but of persons**: Mill here denies that actions can be described as 'brave' or 'benevolent'. This does not follow from the claim that, in any particular case, an action cannot be judged to be good or bad because done by a person who is good or bad, brave or cowardly.

16 **there is nothing in the utilitarian theory inconsistent . . . of their actions**: See the discussion of the Art of Life in *S* 8.949–52; cf. 2.2.2 and n. Mill is correct in so far as certain qualities of character can be assessed according to the pleasure or pain they produce. But since, practically, we can act only to bring about good qualities of character, what matters ultimately to utilitarians in practice will be actions.

18 **The Stoics**: For the Stoic view on virtue and happiness, see Long and Sedley (1987: 368–86, 394–410). The notion that virtue is the only good is, on one interpretation, foreshadowed in Aristotle; see Aristotle (*c*.330 BC/1985: 1098^{a}16–17). For Aristotle, however, it was the exercise rather than the mere possession of virtue which was important.

Paragraph 21

3 **beauties of character**: On the importance of character in assessing consequences of actions, cf. e.g. B 10.98; R 10.7–8; SD 10.56.

6 **moral feelings, but not their sympathies nor their artistic perceptions**: In 5.14–15, Mill distinguishes the sphere of morality from those of 'expediency' and 'worthiness'. This tripartite distinction lines up with the two distinctions in the *System*, between (i) morality, prudence or policy, and aesthetics, and (ii) the right, the expedient, and the beautiful or noble. These distinctions, which are intended to be equivalent, are probably meant to map on to the distinction drawn here. Cf. 2.19.21 and n., 2.20.16 and n., 5.14.10 and n. On the general point that utilitarians have failed to cultivate their sensibilities, see e.g. B 10.89–94.

18 **the moral law**: a Kantian phrase. See e.g. Kant (1785/1995: 5 (389) and *passim*).

Paragraph 22

14 **God desires, above all things, the happiness of his creatures**: This idea of God as impartially benevolent ignores the possibility that God is also just, that is, that he is concerned not only with how much overall happiness there is in the world, but with how it is shared around.

18 **revealed will**: What is revealed by God is to be contrasted with what human beings can discover naturally, by unaided reason.

an utilitarian who believes in the perfect goodness and wisdom of God: The most well-known 'theological utilitarian' was William Paley (1743–1805); see the influential Paley (1785). The argument based on God's benevolence can be found in bk. 2, ch. 5. In the preceding chapter, Paley draws the distinction between the view that God's will is revealed and the view that it must be interpreted. Mill was brought up and remained without religious belief, and blamed customary morality's lacking a consistent principle partly on the failure to face up to contradictions in Christianity (*A* 1.41, 45).

Paragraph 23

5 **the particular interest of the agent himself**: Mill has already stated, in 2.18.1–9, that utilitarianism is concerned with the general happiness, not that of the agent alone.

8 **a rule whose observance is expedient**: See 2.19.39 and n. The two arguments here are: (i) a useful disposition to be honest is damaged by telling a lie; (ii) telling a lie can make people less likely to believe one another, which could be harmful overall. Mill uses a different argument when arguing in *RJ* 31.90 that through association an agent comes to see that if others disobey the laws of justice, he will be destroyed, and that anyone's (including his own) disobeying increases the likelihood of future violations.

28 **possible exceptions**: cf. 5.37.4–11; TS 19.638–40.

acknowledged by all moralists: not strictly correct; some believe that one should tell the truth whatever the consequences.

Paragraph 24

10 **prudence**: i.e. action directed at one's own good.

28 **the received code of ethics is by no means of divine right**: Mill is no conservative. There are many areas of customary morality which should be changed in the light of utilitarianism.

32 **indefinite improvement**: See 2.14.24 and n.

34 **intermediate generalizations**: So we are to pursue the greatest happiness without constant reference to the utilitarian principle, using the rules of customary morality as guides; cf. B 10.110–11; Introd., Sect. 6. After his breakdown, Mill took the view that an individual best achieves his own happiness by not aiming specifically at it (*A* 1.145–7). On the provisionality of rules of conduct, see e.g. *S* 8.946.

46 **the Nautical Almanack**: cf. SD 10.63–6; W 10.180. A suitable analogy, given Mill's recognition above of the imperfect nature of customary morality. Ships went down because of errors in the *Almanac*; see Berger (1984: 314, n. 78).

Paragraph 25

Mill does not properly deal with the temptation objection. It is not merely the claim that utilitarianism allows for practical conflict between moral rules. The difficulty is that the utilitarian, unlike many moralists, sees no genuine moral force in customary morality. It consists merely in 'secondary principles'. Such a view of customary morality might, as a matter of psychological fact, make it more likely that the utilitarian will override it, even when for utilitarian reasons he should not. This, of course, would not be an argument against the truth of utilitarianism.

27 **utility may be invoked to decide**: cf. 1.3.33 and n., 5.26–31.

33 **unacknowledged influence of considerations of utility**: cf. 1.4.5–7.

CHAPTER 3. OF THE ULTIMATE SANCTION OF THE PRINCIPLE OF UTILITY

Paragraph 1

2 **sanction**: a technical term in eighteenth- and nineteenth-century philosophy. Bentham defined sanctions as the sources of the pleasures and pains that motivate people to act (see Bentham 1789/1996: esp. ch. 3; *B* 10.97). For example, because of my physical nature, I shall suffer the pain of hunger if I do not eat; when I do eat, the physical sanction is the source of the pain of hunger and the pleasure of eating. There is also a moral sanction, which consists in popular moral opinions and individual moral approval and disapproval. If I suffer the pain of moral censure, arising out of my desire for a good reputation, the source of my pain is the moral sanction. Sanctions that rested on political authority, including legal sanctions, Bentham puts under the heading of the 'political sanction'. Finally, the religious sanction operates on individuals through their expectation of divine reward and punishment. Bentham was probably influenced here by John Locke (1632–1704); see Locke (1690/1975: bk. 2, ch. 28, sects. 4–13).

what are the motives to obey it?: This is not a merely psychological question. The questioner is asking why he himself **should** feel obliged to promote the general happiness.

15 **the supposed corollaries seem to have a more binding force than the original theorem**: On the relation of particular moral judgements to first principles, cf. 1.2.18–27.

Paragraph 2

1 **the view adopted by the utilitarian philosophy of the nature of the moral sense**: i.e. that the doctrine is false; see 1.3. Mill seems to be assuming that if there is a moral sense, and if it were to detect that utilitarianism is the correct morality, the question of motivation would disappear. But even someone who

believes that utilitarianism is the correct moral theory can ask why he should obey it.

5 **the feeling of unity with our fellow creatures**: The argument is that if I am educated so as to be as concerned about the happiness of others as about my own, I will no longer see any conflict between pursuing self-interest and following utilitarianism. Mill believed that the desires of the good person could overcome, or even silence, other desires. The aim of moral education is to bring people into this state, through educating their desires, and inculcating both a clear understanding of the utilitarian moral standard and a disposition to attend to the morally salient features of situations; see *E* 9.453. Cf. 3.10.

Paragraph 3

3 **external sanctions**: Mill's social sanction is roughly equivalent to Bentham's political and moral sanctions, and Mill takes over the idea of a religious sanction. Within the moral sanction, Bentham included not only actual harm inflicted by others for moral reasons, but the fear of shame and the indignation of others (see Bentham 1789/1996: 12.8, 10). Mill adds to this with his external/internal distinction. External sanctions are not external to the individual; they include the *hope* of favour from others, *fear* of their anger, and *sympathy* for them. But they depend directly on others in a way that the internal sanction does not. External sanctions operate independently of any thought of duty. In introducing the notion of an internal sanction, i.e. pure and unmediated concern for duty, the conscience, Mill was adding elements of Kant and Joseph Butler (1692–1752) to Bentham's view; cf. Kant (1785/1996: 12–14 (397–8)); Butler (1726/1897: vol. 2, sermons 2–3). On Bentham's failure, in Mill's eyes, to understand the conscience, see B 10.95. In 3.10, Mill returns to the external sanction as a natural basis for the internal sanction. The internal sanction has its origins in the influences of others, such as education. But it then takes on a life of its own, providing moral motivation and concern which is independent of any other-regarding motivation and concern; cf. B 10.13–16.

10 **those of them which refer to our fellow creatures**: The argument here is that, once one realizes that others place as much importance on their happiness as one does on one's own, one will see that promoting the happiness of others is the best way to seek favour from them, and to benefit them in so far as one is sympathetic with them.

17 **the goodness of God**: cf. 2.22.18 and n.

18 **the essence, or even only the criterion, of good**: For Mill, it is really only the criterion, or the mark, of the good in question. The essence of the good, what makes it good, is its pleasurableness. As an empiricist, however, Mill was inclined not to give much metaphysical content to the notion of essence.

21 **physical**: sheer bodily pleasure and pain.

Notes: Chapter 3

Paragraph 4

6 **the pure idea of duty**: Mill is here speaking of a concern to do one's duty—whatever it is—for its own sake.

13 **self-abasement**: Mill's views on the nature of morality have much in common with those of the German philosopher, Friedrich Nietzsche (1844–1900); cf. e.g. Nietzsche (1886/1966: 101–2).
extreme complication: Because of the complexity of the compound of concern for duty with sympathetic and other associations, people fail to see moral obligation for what it is and assume that it cannot be attached to anything independent of customary morality.

Paragraph 5

2 **subjective feeling**: See next paragraph. A subjective feeling is one which is not a response to any objective fact. Mill's naturalism did not allow him to believe in normative facts, facts about reasons for action.

3 **those whose standard is utility**: On utilitarianism and the conscience, cf. W 10.172, 178–9.

Paragraph 6

2 **a transcendental fact**: Mill is referring here to the intuitionists, especially those such as Whewell influenced by Kant's transcendental idealism; cf. 2.17.3. The notion of 'things in themselves' is Kantian; see e.g. Kant (1787/1950: 74 (B 45) and *passim*).

6 **Ontology**: The philosophy of what exists. *On*, in ancient Greek, means 'being'.

11 **so far as it is disinterested**: The implication is that the external sanctions do not emerge from the purely impartial moral point of view.

12 **the notion therefore of the transcendental moralists**: No good reason is offered for ascribing this strong view to the intuitionists.

18 **But is this danger confined to the utilitarian morality?**: This passage and the following paragraph are the places in *Utilitarianism* in which Mill seems most aware of the distinction between first- and second-order ethical questions (questions, respectively, within ethics and about ethics). His argument here deflects the issue nicely, so that the weakness of the next argument (see next n.) is not a serious problem. See the final sentence of 3.7 for a concise statement of the strong argument.

19 **Does the belief . . . external sanctions**: The argument here is not entirely persuasive. The objection was not that objectivists will never question their conscience, but that they are less likely to. The claim that, once one has

129

questioned one's conscience, it will be the external sanctions and not belief in objectivism that lead one to respect it, not only is implausible, but fails as a response to the original objection.

Paragraph 7

4 **intuitive perception is of principles**: cf. 1.3.3–15.
7 **regard to the pleasures and pains of others**: cf. 3.10.
12 **a large *portion* of morality**: cf. 1.4.12 and n.

Paragraph 8

1 **the moral feelings are not innate, but acquired**: Again Mill follows an Aristotelian line; cf. Aristotle (*c.*330 BC/1985: bk. 2, ch. 1). On the natural growth of the moral sentiments and against the claim that virtue is innate, see also *E* 9.454–60; EG 22.7–9; Letter to W. G. Ward (1849) 14.30.

Paragraph 9

2 **dissolving force of analysis**: cf. *A* 1.141, 143.

Paragraph 10

1 **natural sentiment**: In his view of sympathy as natural, Mill shows the influence of David Hume (1711–76); cf. Hume (1739–40/1978: bk. 3, pt. 3, sect. 1); Hume (1751/1975: sect. 9, pt. 1, paras. 222–3); SD 10.60–1. Sympathy is to be distinguished from the sense of duty; see *R* 10.13.
6 **tend to become stronger**: On Mill's belief in progress, see 2.14.24 and n. On progress towards equality in particular, see *SW* 21.272–3 and *passim*. The one exception to this progress of civilization, Mill believed, was the relation between the sexes, which remained highly unequal.
35 **to identify his *feelings* more and more with their good**: On the education of self-interest, cf. CC 26.324.
58 **religion**: cf. 3.3. Mill saw utilitarianism as his religion: *A* 1.69. To understand Mill's view of the role of religion in moral education, one must read UR 10.403–28; on the power of education, see 10.409.
65 **Comte**: Auguste Comte, French political philosopher and father of sociology (1798–1857). Comte (1851–4) advocates a capitalist dictatorship, based on the spiritual power of science. On Comte in general, see *AC* 10.261–368; on Comte on religion without god, focusing on the general interest, see *AC* 10.332–5. For more on Mill on the 'religion of humanity', see *D* 27.646; Letter to Comte (1842) 13.560; T 10.488–9; UR 10.410–15, 420–6.
69 **psychical**: changed from 'psychological' in the 2nd edn.

74 **human freedom and individuality**: Mill's concern for the effect of social custom on individuality emerges especially in *On Liberty*; see esp. *L* 18.219–21.

Paragraph 11

5 **entireness of sympathy**: On one interpretation, Mill is here suggesting that human beings may become completely impartial between their own interests and those of others.

16 **denounce and defy**: Mill allows that in certain cases of 'depravation of taste' we are entitled to criticize the ways of life of others in their own interests; see *L* 18.278.

24 **it would not be well for them to be without**: On the moral sentiments as higher pleasures, see 2.4.18–19, 6.7–8, 9.9–13.

CHAPTER 4. OF WHAT SORT OF PROOF THE PRINCIPLE OF UTILITY IS SUSCEPTIBLE

Paragraph 1

1 **It has already been remarked**: See 1.5.4–6.

2 **proof**: 'The proofs of the moral and social truths of greatest importance to mankind, are few, brief, and easily intelligible' (SA 22.242); '[m]oral regenerators in this age mostly aim at setting up a new form either of Stoicism or of Puritanism—persuading men to sink altogether earthly happiness as a pursuit. . . . What is now wanted is the creed of Epicurus warmed by the additional element of an enthusiastic love of the general good' (D 27.666).

3 **first premises of our knowledge**: As an empiricist, Mill believed that all knowledge rests on the evidence of the senses. My knowledge that at least some grass is green rests e.g. on my having experienced green grass. And, though reason alone cannot prove this claim, I can prove this to you, in a rational way, by showing you some. His aim is to put ethics on the same basis as empirical science: England's 'thinkers are again beginning to see what they had only temporarily forgotten, that a true Psychology is the indispensable scientific basis of Morals' (*E* 9.2); cf. fn. to 5.36.25. His argument should be read alongside that in Bentham (1789 / 1996: chs. 1–2).

6 **internal consciousness**: e.g. memory. I might try to remind you of the grass you sat on last week.

Paragraph 2

1 **ends . . . what things are desirable**: Strictly, this is not so. What is desirable is what is worth desiring, and it may be that some ends—some goods or goals worth achieving—can best be achieved by not desiring them. Happiness itself

is an example, as Mill knew; see *A* 1.145, 147. But this is not a serious problem for Mill's argument, since what is desired reflectively for itself is usually assumed to be an end in the sense of being something good.

2 **The utilitarian doctrine**: More accurately, the doctrine is that the *general* happiness is the only thing desirable; cf. 1.1.16 and n.

Paragraph 3

1 **visible . . . desirable**: Mill's keenness for an analogy between belief and desire, as sources of evidence for matters of fact and ultimate ends respectively, led him into a lack of clarity which cost his reputation dearly (see esp. Moore (1903: sects. 40–1)). 'Visible' means 'can be desired', whereas 'desirable', as the previous paragraph itself implies, means 'worth desiring'. Mill's argument can be appreciated through interpolation: 'the sole evidence it is possible to produce [for people] that anything is desirable, is that [those] people do actually desire it'.

8 **No reason can be given . . . a good to the aggregate of all persons**: Again, serious problems of interpretation arise in this passage because of Mill's failure, which emerges in the very first paragraph of *Utilitarianism*, to recognize the importance of the distinction between egoistic and universalistic or impartial hedonism (i.e. utilitarianism). (He is well aware of the distinction itself; cf. e.g. SD 10.71.) If you admit that you desire your own happiness, I am well on the way to persuading you that your own happiness is desirable. But Mill appears to be saying that this is the only reason I can offer to persuade you that the happiness of all, the total amount of happiness in the world, is desirable, i.e. something worthy of desire, an end. The argument 'that each person's happiness is a good to that person, and the general happiness, therefore, a good to the aggregate of all persons' confuses things further, since the general happiness is here implied to be an end not for an individual, but for an aggregate. The conclusion Mill requires is that the general happiness is a good or an end to *each* person (and, indeed, one that is not in competition, in the case of each person, with their own happiness). Is that what he means? Henry Jones thought so, but Mill rebutted his suggestion in a letter:

As to the sentence you quote from my 'Utilitarianism'; when I said the general happiness is a good to the aggregate of all persons I did not mean that every human being's happiness is a good to every other human being, though I think, in a good state of society and education it would be so. I merely meant in this particular sentence to argue that since A's happiness is a good, B's a good, C's a good, &c., the sum of all these goods must be a good. ((1868) 16.1414)

The claim that 'every human being's happiness is a good to every other' Mill almost certainly sees as equivalent to 'the sum of all individual happinesses is a good to each human being'. Strictly, his last sentence in the passage quoted is a logical fallacy—the so-called fallacy of composition, committed when one ascribes to a set what is true of its members. Here are three large people; but a set of three people is not large. But we can see what Mill means: good is additive, in that two people's (equal) goods contain twice as much goodness, other things being equal, as either of them taken alone. What Mill needs in his argument to prove utilitarianism, however, is exactly what he denies in this letter that that argument contains, for the egoist could agree with Mill's additive assumptions, but deny that goodness translates directly into the rationality of ends. That is, he can claim that, even though he could bring about the greatest good by acting in some way, this is not what is most *desirable for him* as an end. Rather, what is most desirable for him is his own greatest happiness. Mill needs an argument for impartiality; see fn. to 5.36.

Paragraph 4

5 **virtue**: Mill chooses this example because it was the most likely to be employed by his intuitionist 'opponents of the utilitarian standard'. For example, Whewell argued that virtue, though it produces enjoyment, is not identical with it (Whewell 1837: 59–60).

Paragraph 5

4 **Whatever may be the opinion of utilitarian moralists**: Mill's own associationist account is in the following two paragraphs.

7 **another end than virtue**: i.e. the greatest overall balance of pleasure over pain.

19 **The ingredients of happiness**: Mill again shows the influence of Aristotle's 'inclusive' conception of happiness, and it is important to note that Aristotle sees the exercise of virtue as constituting happiness: see Aristotle (*c.330* BC/1985: 1097^{b}14–20, 1098^{a}16–17). Cf. also Hartley (1749: vol. 1, ch. 4, sect. 6); James Mill (1829: 294); Whewell (1845: 356).

21 **any given pleasure**: This phrase shows that Mill is here thinking of the *pleasure* of being virtuous, i.e. the pleasure of acting virtuously or of the consciousness of one's own virtue; see 4.8.5–7; cf. W 10.184 n. On association and pleasure, cf. AP 31.221, 229, 231–2; R 10.13; SD 10.62. For Mill's proof to succeed, he must be taken to be speaking of the pleasure of virtue, not virtue itself.

22 **exemption from pain**: Mill is again unclear here about pleasure and pain; cf. 2.2.16 and n. Health can be desired for itself either as a relief from pain or as something the consciousness of which is pleasurable; as sheer exemption from pain, however, it is a mere means, not something desirable in itself.

Notes: Chapter 4

Paragraph 6

3 **by association**: Mill's explanation is fully grounded in the associationist psychology he inherited from Bentham and his father (see Hartley 1749: vol. 1, ch. 1; James Mill 1829: chs. 3, 22). In the *System of Logic*, Mill speaks of the 'second Law of Association': '[W]hen two impressions have been frequently experienced (or even thought of), either simultaneously or in immediate succession, then whenever one of these impressions, or the idea of it, recurs, it tends to excite the idea of the other' (*S* 8.852). Thus, I originally use money to buy food, which provides me with certain 'primitive pleasures'. Then, by association, I come to desire the pleasure of possessing money as an end in itself. The same associationist story can be told about pain; cf. 4.7.3; *E* 9.455.

5 **love of money**: cf. James Mill (1829: 218); Bain (1859: 320). James Mill says that money is '[an] instance commonly adduced' in this context.

39 **primitive desires**: For the claim that bodily pleasures provide the foundation for higher pleasures, see Hartley (1749: vol. 2, 213).

Paragraph 8

6 **the consciousness of being without it**: i.e. the unpleasant awareness of lack of virtue is part of unhappiness. Mill allows that one could desire virtue merely to relieve the pain of this unpleasant awareness, but does not recognize that such a person would not be desiring virtue for its own sake, as a good in itself, but merely as a means to avoid something bad in itself. On motivation by pleasure and pain, see R 10.12–13.

Paragraph 9

1 **the question, of what sort of proof**: Mill runs two projects in tandem in this chapter: (i) an account of what sort of proof can be given of utilitarianism; (ii) a version of such a proof.

7 **the promotion**: i.e. overall happiness should be maximized.

9 **a part is included in the whole**: Mill saw morality as just one sphere of human conduct, the other two being Prudence and Aesthetics; cf. 2.2.2 and n., 5.14.10 and n.; *S* 8.949. The 'ultimate' principle is equivalent, practically, to the utilitarian principle, since it enjoins the maximization of happiness; but it will not be stated in moral terms.

Paragraph 10

3 **a question of fact and experience**: as are all questions, ultimately, for an empiricist; cf. 4.1.3 and n.

7 **desiring a thing and finding it pleasant**: Mill's language here is loose. An intuitionist who claimed that we desire virtue as a non-hedonistic good could agree that we nevertheless find virtue pleasant. Likewise, he could agree with the claim at the end of the paragraph that we desire anything 'only in proportion as the idea of it is pleasant', but suggest that we nevertheless desire items such as virtue on the ground that they possess certain non-hedonistic properties.

11 **to think of an object as desirable**: This phrase suggests that Mill's proof does not consist solely in an appeal to desire, but to a belief concerning what is desirable, i.e., he says, pleasant; cf. the notion of 'deliberate preference', 4.11.23. Again, it seems that Mill must be assuming that what are desired are pleasurable experiences. In *S* 8.842, Mill allows that one can desire an action independently of pleasure. But the context makes clear that he is here thinking of *will*, which at 4.11.12 he distinguishes from desire. On the idea that desire is the idea of a pleasure associated with the future, see *AP* 31.215. Mill says there that he thinks that in '[d]esire there is . . . always included a positive stimulation to action'; cf. *AP* 31.251.

12 **one and the same thing**: This is too strong, since it clearly makes sense to say that one thinks that something is desirable *because* it is pleasant. Mill's claim need be only that this is the sole reason people find anything desirable; and it is this claim which his opponents will refuse to accept.

14 **metaphysical**: i.e. 'psychological'; cf. 4.9.3. Mill of all people would not have appealed to introspection to decide on metaphysical possibility; see *E* 9.66–9.

Paragraph 11

In this paragraph, Mill accepts that individuals act virtuously with no thought of the pleasure of so doing. But, he suggests, they are acting not from desire, but from will, engendered by habit. So this phenomenon is not a counter-example to the proof. Nor is such behaviour to be discouraged, because of its instrumental conduciveness to happiness.

11 **have stated it elsewhere**: *S* 8.842–3.

24 **Third and last**: Examples of the three types of case might be: (i) a person unthinkingly gives a beggar a coin out of habit; (ii) a person who has decided she wishes to be generous nevertheless consciously turns away from a beggar out of habit; (iii) a person committed to virtue consciously gives a beggar a coin out of habit.

33 **desire only because we will it**: e.g. a person may desire to give a coin to a beggar (i.e. desire the pleasure of giving a coin to a beggar), the explanation of why she so desires in this case being that she has developed a habit of giving to others.

40 **by making the person *desire* virtue—by making him think of it in a**

pleasurable light: For stress on the importance of desiring the right pleasures in moral education, see Aristotle (*c*.330 BC/1985: bk. 2, ch. 1).

49 **no presumption of being intrinsically good**: because habit is, by definition, unthinking, whereas desire—at least for ultimate ends—rests on the belief that something is good. 'Intrinsically', here, means 'in itself', or 'non-instrumentally'.

53 **the support of habit**: For virtue as consisting in a firm disposition, see Aristotle (*c*.330 BC/1985: 1105ᵃ28–33).

58 **this state of will is a means to good, not intrinsically a good**: *pace* Kant (1785/1995: 9 (393)).

Paragraph 12

2 **the consideration of the thoughtful reader**: Mill's strategy in this chapter is to encourage each reader to ask themselves what they ultimately desire, believing that the evidence thus provided will persuade each that only pleasure is desirable.

CHAPTER 5. ON THE CONNEXION BETWEEN JUSTICE AND UTILITY

Paragraph 1

3 **Justice**: cf. e.g. Bain (1859: 306). The problem is that utilitarianism often appears to require injustice, as when e.g. it will maximize utility to punish an innocent person or for goods to be distributed unfairly.

6 **an inherent quality in things**: According to Mill, the proponents of anti-utilitarian justice claim that, because our beliefs about justice seem self-evident, they must be a response to a moral reality independent of those beliefs and any of our sentiments. A proponent of justice need not take this line. He could, for the sake of argument, agree with Mill about the nature of ethics and the origin of our moral beliefs, but continue to advocate a principle of justice in opposition to utilitarianism.

9 **never, in the long run, disjoined from it in fact**: Mill believes that utilitarianism requires us to abide by 'secondary principles' of justice, since, even if these do not maximize the good in each case, in the long run they will produce the best results; cf. 2.24, 5.2.24–6, 5.32.3.

Paragraph 2

1 **no necessary connexion**: Mill is clear here about the distinction between first- and second-order ethical questions. In this paragraph, he suggests that his aim in ch. 5 is not to criticize objectivist views of ethics, which he distanced

himself from in 3.6–8, but to enquire first into whether justice, or rather our feelings of justice, can be accounted for in such a way that no threat to utilitarianism arises from the power of the notion of justice.

16 **Our present object**: cf. *A* 1.269: 'The practical reformer has continually to demand that changes be made in things which are supported by powerful and widely spread feelings, or to question the apparent necessity and indefeasibleness of established facts; and it is often an indispensable part of his argument to shew, how those powerful feelings had their origin, and how those facts came to seem necessary and indefeasible.' Cf. R 10.6; SD 10.57.

22 *sui generis*: i.e. in its own special class.

27 **subjective mental feeling of Justice . . . simple expediency**: e.g. we shall be far more inclined to blame someone for an injustice than for failing to bring about the greatest happiness. Mill accepts that at present utilitarianism is not attached to any strong sentiment (3.1). Indeed, according to him, his breakdown at the age of 20 was brought on by his being unmoved by the prospect of utilitarianism's being universally accepted and practised (*A* 1.139).

Paragraph 3

13 **a special provision of Nature**: and so, perhaps, a 'revelation of some objective reality' (5.2.15–16).

15 **the main problem**: Mill suggests that the main problem is the question of the origin of the sentiment of justice; in fact, however, the main problem is whether justice poses a problem for utilitarianism. Our sentiments' being explicable does not require that their deliverances be ignored. Indeed, Mill's proof rests on an appeal to our desires. We see later that Mill's real project is to show that the sentiment has its origin in utilitarian considerations; cf. 5.16.5–6.

Paragraph 5

9 **we shall return**: See 5.8.6–9.

Paragraph 6

8 **(which condemns . . . against them)**: Mill here speaks implicitly in favour of civil disobedience.

18 **all laws which are inexpedient are unjust**: This is of course the view of Bentham and other utilitarians; see e.g. Bentham (1789/1996: 10.40 n. b2).

Paragraph 7

2 **unjust that he should obtain a good**: The previous sentence implies that it is also unjust that someone should fail to receive a good or an evil which he deserves.

4 **clearest and most emphatic form**: This is because, Mill will argue, of the origin of our sentiments of justice in the desire to inflict harm.
7 **good if he does right**: Mill speaks here only of moral desert, leaving to one side cases in which, for example, people are said to deserve success if they have worked hard. The 'general sense' allows for cosmic injustice, as when e.g. a great benefactor of humanity is killed by an avalanche.
10 **returning good for evil**: Mill is thinking here of the Christian doctrine that one should love one's enemies.

Paragraph 8

1 **an engagement**: The obvious example here is promising.
2 **express or implied, or disappoint expectations raised by our own conduct**: e.g. I might say, 'I promise I'll be at the Rose and Crown at 6 o'clock'; or, in answer to your question about whether I am coming, 'I plan to be there'; or I might have met you there every evening for the last six months, and not said anything about not turning up this evening.
3 **knowingly and voluntarily**: cf. Aristotle (*c*.330 BC/1985: 1109^{b}35–1110^{a}4). It is not unjust for me not to turn up at the Rose and Crown if I unknowingly (and, we may assume, non-culpably) led you to believe that I would be there, or if you coerced me into agreeing to be there.
5 **not regarded as absolute**: See 5.37.4–14.
6 **a stronger obligation of justice**: e.g. I may have promised that I will be at the Rose and Crown, having forgotten my vital role in a very important legal case concerning someone's entitlements.
8 **a *forfeiture***: After your rudeness to me after the meeting, you have no right to expect that I am going to turn up at six o'clock.

Paragraph 9

4 **not . . . a duty in itself**: Impartiality, Mill explains, is sometimes a matter of rights (the 1st and 2nd spheres), and sometimes a matter of desert (the 4th sphere). And there are other grounds for impartiality, such as concern for the public rather than the private interest.
8 **no superiority in good offices**: and such partiality can be the most effective way of promoting the greatest happiness.

Paragraph 10

1 **Nearly allied to the idea of impartiality**: People e.g. with equal rights or of equal deservingness should be treated impartially, that is, equally.
5 **always conforms . . . to their notion of utility**: an exaggeration, at the very least. Mill is here engaging in some rather implausible armchair moral psy-

chological explanations, presumably based on his view that the principle of utility, although hidden, underlies 'steady' moral beliefs (see 1.4.5–14). In fact, many of those who accept a principle of equality believe that there are cases in which this principle should override any version of the general happiness principle. For example, one might believe that slaves should be freed even if it is clear that this will bring down the total amount of overall happiness.

25 **whose needs are greatest**: 'needs' replaced 'wants' in the 2nd edn.

28 **the sense of natural justice**: i.e. we can all see the force of an appeal to justice in favour of equal distribution, distribution according to need, and so on.

Paragraph 11

2 **the mental link which holds them together**: Mill is assuming that, since the term 'justice' is not ambiguous, its various different senses must have something in common. An opponent might suggest that, in fact, there is nothing common to all usages, but only 'family-resemblances' between sets; see Wittgenstein (1958: pt. 1, sect. 67).

6 **etymology**: cf. N 10.396.

Paragraph 12

This paragraph as a whole was one of those most changed by Mill in later editions of *Utilitarianism*.

2 **points to an origin**: was 'points distinctly to an origin' in *Fraser's* and 1st edn.

4 *Justum*: Latin, 'justice'. Latest scholarship suggests that the root, *ius*, is related not to the verb 'to order', but to the Sanskrit *yoh*, 'healthy', or the Aventan *yaož-dadaiti*, 'purifies'; see Glare (1982: 977, 984). But it is important to note that the plausibility of Mill's argument concerning the relation between justice and punishment does not rest solely on the etymological claims in this paragraph.

5 **Δίκαιον**: Greek, 'justice'. Even in its earliest uses, δίκη could be used to refer to what is just or right (see e.g. Homer, *Iliad*, bk. 19, l.180), and even opposed to mere force (*Iliad* 16.388). Mill's view that notions of the authoritative in early societies were based on force is also found in his account of the origin of morality in SW 21.264–70. Mill's account of justice as originally a system to rationalize oppression has something in common with Karl Marx's view of bourgeois justice; see esp. Marx (1964). Marx's influence on Mill was, however, negligible.

9 *Recht*: German for 'right'. For meanings, see Wildhagen and Hérancourt (1972: vol. 2, 1002, s.v.).

12 *wrong*: See Murray *et al.* (1928: 387, s.v.).

Latin equivalents: Mill has in mind *pravus* and, perhaps, *erro*. This is not true of many Latin words for 'wrong', such as *malus*.

20 **established term for judicature**: Mill included a fn. in *Fraser's* and the 1st edn. at this point: 'I am not committing the fallacy imputed with some show of truth to Horne Tooke, of assuming that a word must still continue to mean what it originally meant. Etymology is slight evidence of what the idea now signified is, but the very best evidence of how it sprang up.' John Horne Tooke (1736–1812) was a Radical politician and nominalist philosopher.

21 *idée mère*: literally, 'mother idea'.

32 **violations of such laws as *ought* to exist**: For the distinction between what is just by convention and just by nature, see Aristotle (*c.*330 BC / 1985: bk. 5, ch. 7). The distinction here maps on to that between the first two spheres of justice (5.5–6).

Paragraph 13

4 **the whole detail of private life**: e.g. my promise to meet you at the Rose and Crown.

9 **we do not always think it expedient**: Mill again imputes a subliminal belief in utilitarianism to everyone; cf. 1.4.5–14, 5.10.5 and n.

20 **our own and the public disapprobation**: Mill sees voiced moral disapproval as a form of punishment, based on the unpleasantness of being blamed. This unpleasantness is caused by the moral sentiment which rests on our desire to be at one with our fellows; see 3.10.

Paragraph 14

6 **We do not call anything wrong . . . of his own conscience**: This paragraph is one of the most discussed in recent Mill scholarship, many writers claiming that it represents a move away from utilitarianism. Such an interpretation is strongly to be resisted: Mill himself tells us that he remained a utilitarian throughout his life, 2.2 almost certainly contains a commitment to utilitarianism, and this chapter is an attempt to reconcile justice with utilitarianism. It is important to remember the context of this paragraph. Mill is attempting to analyse the nature and origin of our sentiments of justice and of moral obligation, and in that sense is working at the second-order level—answering questions about ethics, rather than within ethics itself. According to Mill, when I say, 'This action is wrong', I mean, 'This action ought to be punished, by law, opinion, or conscience' (cf. Bain 1859: 286).

Some have claimed that a philosopher's meta-ethical statements and their first-order ethical statements should be seen as isolated from one another. But there seems little justification for this claim. So Mill must be said to believe that when he says, 'Actions which fail to maximize happiness are wrong', he means, 'Actions which fail to maximize happiness should be punished by law, opinion, or conscience'. But what of a case in which punishing a non-maximizing action would itself not maximize happiness? Mill must surely rule out punishment by law or opinion, since legal action and blaming are *actions*, and non-maximizing actions are wrong. However, he can accept that punishment by conscience ought always to follow non-maximizing actions, *even when* this does not maximize utility. This has the odd consequence that there may be cases in which something ought to be the case—your being punished by your conscience—but I should not act to bring it about, by, say, reminding you of what you did, for my so acting would itself be a failure to maximize.

Further difficulties arise when we recall that Mill believes that—for sound utilitarian reasons—our moral life should be dominated not by utilitarianism, but by customary morality. A conscience which has developed within customary morality, as Mill accepts (3.1), will lead to guilt feelings not at failure to maximize happiness, but at failure to live up to customary morality. And that is how Mill thinks things should be. The only solution here is to assume that Mill moves from one discourse to another, from the theoretical to the practical. At the theoretical level, what he thinks is 'really' wrong is failure to maximize utility. But those sets of actions which maximize will include accepting and abiding, in most cases, by customary morality. So the right action in any case will be that action in the set of future actions which maximizes happiness, and that is likely to be the set in accordance with customary morality. In most cases, therefore, utilitarianism and customary morality coincide in their deliverances as to whether blame is appropriate.

Mill's project here is naturalistic and reductive. He wishes to explain the phenomenon of morality without postulating the objective existence of peculiar properties such as 'wrongness', or 'responsibility'. All we need to account for the distinction between moral good and evil, he believes, is to recognize that humanity will encourage those who benefit them, and demonstrate aversion to those who harm them (*E* 9.456). But are moral guilt and the fear of disapproval not quite distinct? Mill has this to say in a letter to W. G. Ward of 1859:

The pains of conscience are certainly very different from those of dread of disapprobation; yet it might well be, that the innumerable associations of pain with doing wrong which have been rivetted by a long succession of pains undergone, or pains feared or imagined as the consequence of wrong things done, or of wrong things which we have been tempted to do (especially in early life), may produce a general and intense feeling of recoil from wrongdoing in which no conscious influence of other people's disapprobation may be perceptible. (15.649)

This letter as a whole is important in interpreting 5.14. Later, Mill says that conscience is anyway not to be understood solely in terms of a model of fear of disapproval. I feel conscious that if I violate moral laws, others will naturally feel that I should be punished. I then put myself in their position, and sympathize with their desire. The painfulness of not being at one with them leads me to refrain from violations of moral laws.

A serious question arises whether any such reductive account of morality 'unmasks' or debunks it to the point where first-order moral judgements can be seen only as expressions of taste.

10 **morality and simple expediency**: Mill is here thinking of two spheres of his 'Art of Life'; cf. 2.2.2 and n., 2.19.21 and n., 2.20.16 and n., 5.15.16. In one sphere, we speak of what duty requires, and we blame those who do wrong by failing to do their duty. In the other spheres, we admire or criticize people for doing or not doing certain things, or for possessing certain characteristics, but blame is absent: 'it was very good of you to bring this book back so promptly'; 'she's a bit of a misery'. The first is the sphere of 'compulsion', the second the sphere of 'persuasion' (5.14.29). This distinction corresponds to that between duty and doing what is beyond the call of duty (*supererogation*) (cf. Bain 1859: 322). The sphere of supererogation within customary morality itself rests on utilitarianism, in that it is for the general good that in certain areas of life people's behaviour be left more or less up to them: TL 5.650–1. Into the category of persuasion Mill puts virtue, which should be praised as heroism (Letters to H. S. Brandreth and E. W. Young (1867) 16.1234, 1327–8).

22 **in the sequel**: See esp. 5.19–25, 32–7.

30 **Professor Bain** (fn.): Alexander Bain (1818–1903), a disciple of Mill. The reference here is to Bain (1859: ch. 15). Though the linking of punishment and moral obligation by Bain was 'nothing new', Mill believed that his presentation of the associationist position was the best (BP 11.364). Bain's chapter contains many ideas in common with Mill's.

Paragraph 15

6 **perfect and . . . imperfect obligation**: the terms are Kantian; see Kant (1785/ 1995: 38 (421)). The origin of the distinction is in the natural law tradition, especially Hugo Grotius (1583–1645) and Samuel Pufendorf (1632–94).

12 **correlative *right***: Mill's conception of justice is very broad; see Introd., Sect. 9. For the idea that perfect obligations correlate with rights, see Bain (1859: 323); Bain himself refers to Paley.

Paragraph 16

4 **whether it could have grown up**: The idea of justice is the idea of perfect obligation with correlative rights. Mill's question is whether this very idea could have given rise to the sentiment attached to it. There is something odd about this, since the idea of obligation itself has been said to involve the sentiment. Mill's real question, however, is whether the sentiment could have

arisen naturally and out of utilitarian considerations, not whether it came from the idea itself.

Paragraph 17

3 **whatever is moral in it**: This is an interesting example of Mill's switching discourses. On the one hand, he wishes to characterize morality, or rather that part of it that consists in talk of perfect obligations, in terms of the sentiment of justice. But he is then ready to stand back from the sentiment and his analysis, and assess it from the moral point of view he himself accepts, namely, utilitarianism. It is then, of course, no surprise that 'what is moral' in the sentiment of justice is what coincides with utilitarianism.

Paragraph 18

1 **two essential ingredients**: See 5.13–14 and 5.15 respectively.
2 **the desire to punish**: more precisely, the desire that such a person be punished. 5.13 suggested that our first wish is that the person be punished by the courts. Mill's shifting of the focus to the desire to punish makes his claim in the following paragraphs that the origin of this desire lies in the impulse of self-defence appear more plausible.

Paragraph 20

1 **It is natural to resent**: Mill believed that the sentiment of justice has arisen because of our need for it. If *rewarding* offenders for refraining from crime turned out to be more effective, the sentiment would die away; E 9.460n. For the idea that resentment is central to morality, see Bain (1859: 180–1).
7 **in being capable of sympathizing**: The role of natural sympathy in the foundations of ethics had been stressed by many previous philosophers; see esp. the sympathy-based accounts of Adam Smith and David Hume, both of whom emphasize the advantages to general happiness of principles of justice; see e.g. Hume (1751/1975: sects. 3 and 5); Smith (1759/1976: bk. 2, sect. 2, ch. 2).
8 **some of the more noble animals**: Mill would not have included his cat 'Puss', who appeared to him to have forgotten him entirely when he returned from a trip to France; see Letter to Helen Taylor (1860) 15.660.
10 **a more developed intelligence**: This works in two ways. First, in a 'self-regarding' way, I recognize that society's security depends on morality's being respected, and that a threat to that ground of security is a threat to my own self-interest. Secondly, in a 'sympathetic' way, just as a mother animal sympathizes with her young, so I sympathize with the collectivity protected by morality, and am roused to defend that collectivity. For more on this

explanation, see n. on 5.22.5. Sympathy, Mill believes, is not to be collapsed into self-interest, in that the pleasures and pains of sympathy are not 'consciously referred to self' (*AP* 31.219; cf. *AP* 31.232).

Paragraph 21

5 **has nothing moral in it**: Here again we see Mill shifting discourses, from talk *about* the institution of morality, to talk *within* morality. It is, on the face of it, odd to say that the sentiment of justice has nothing moral in it, for Mill has been explaining this sentiment as a moral sentiment. But what he means here is that there is nothing morally admirable in this sentiment, in itself. What is morally admirable is the sentiment's working to promote 'the general good'. So Mill is ready to assess the moral sentiments, considered as natural artefacts, from the point of view which rests upon those sentiments themselves. The problem is that his opponents will disagree with him at this very point.

10 **conformable to the general good**: Presumably, given that he is attempting to explain the role of justice in customary morality, Mill means '*thought* conformable to the general good'. Likewise, we should presumably understand 'they believe that' before 'society' in line 12.

11 **not resenting a hurt to themselves**: A just person will not e.g. resent others doing better than him in a competitive examination, even though this harms him, because society has no interest in preventing such harm—indeed, quite the opposite. See *L* 18.292–3.

Paragraph 22

5 **a person whose resentment is really a moral feeling**: Mill now uses his account of the origin of morality to rule out as non-moral the sentiments of those who do not feel that moral rules are for the benefit of others. The sentiment of those who resent the violation of rules for any other reason is not 'really a moral feeling'. It is, perhaps, a mere response to pain inflicted on oneself, or just a gut reaction. There are at least two responses available to Mill's intuitionist opponent at this point. First, Mill could be said to be just wrong about the role of morality. In fact, the moral rules are not for anyone's *benefit*; rather, they are self-standing requirements or constraints, the violators of which deserve punishment or blame for their violation itself. The parenthesis in lines 10–11, if epexegetic, and the discussion of Kant below suggest that Mill did not even conceive of such a view. His view is that 'rules of action . . . must take their whole character and colour from the end to which they are subservient' (1.2.21–3). Respecting moral rules cannot, for him, be an end in itself. Secondly, he could be accused of a form of genetic fallacy. The moral sentiments perhaps do have their origin in the impulse of self-defence sympathetically extended, but it may be that from the point of view which

they make possible we can see that the content of morality does not itself have to make reference to the interests of others. Finally, a moral nihilist or sceptic may argue that Mill has in fact explained morality away. If it is just a matter of natural, albeit intellectualized and extended, sentiment, what reason does that give me to respect it? Here Mill must return to the arguments of chapter 3, and attempt to ground moral behaviour on self-interest. But he himself is well aware of the limitations of this approach in society as it is.

13 **Kant**: See 1.4.23 and n.

19 **a rule even of utter selfishness ... rational beings**: Mill misses the importance of the notion of will in the Kantian system. 'You can will' must be inserted before 'thy rule of conduct' in Mill's formulation. Kant is quite aware that a society could function on the basis of selfishness, but argues that one could not rationally will this because it would rule out that help which one would want oneself from others; see Kant (1785/1975: 40 (423)). In this case, the agent's will is constrained not by the interests of others but by his own. It might be argued that Kant builds into his general account of rationality a concern for the interests of others which does not emerge out of 'pure reason'. But that would be an argument different from Mill's here.

Paragraph 23

3 **common to all mankind**: i.e. a rule which everyone should accept. This implies that a relativist's sentiments are not 'really' moral either.

12 **its peculiar impressiveness**: Because the strong impulse of self-defence lies behind justice, and utilitarianism lacks the support of the sentiments (3.1), it has not been recognized, Mill will go on to argue, that justice in fact has a basis in utility. .

Paragraph 24

8 **When we call anything a person's right, we mean that he has a valid claim**: This analysis is likely to be generally accepted by all sides. The difference will emerge in views about what *makes* the claim valid. Some will argue that the claim is valid *because* he has a right, and that the right is the fundamental ground of the claim. Mill, however, will go on to suggest that having a right is *nothing other than* having a valid claim, so that the validity of the claim must rest on something other than rights, namely, of course, utility.

Paragraph 25

4 **does not seem to convey a sufficient feeling**: cf. 3.1.

5 **energy of the feeling**: 'energy of the sentiment' in *Fraser's*.

10 **security**: The stress on adherence to morality as the basis for security is

strongly reminiscent of the argument in *Leviathan* by Thomas Hobbes (1588–1679) that the moral virtues lead to peace and the preservation of oneself and of society; see esp. Hobbes (1651/1968: pt. 1, ch. 17). See also Bain (1859: 304–5) (Bain refers to Paley). Cf. *AP* 31.241–2.

22 **gathers feelings round it**: This is associationism again; cf. 3.10.11, 46.

30 *ought* **and** *should* **grow into** *must*: Mill is here attempting to explain the common belief that moral reasons are overriding.

31 **a moral necessity, analogous to physical, and often not inferior to it in binding force**: Mill believes that morality is a coercive social force, the operation of which is justified because of its promotion of happiness.

Paragraph 26

4 **why that internal oracle is so ambiguous**: Mill's argument in these paragraphs is slightly tricksy (cf. TL 5.650–1). He suggests that, if there were a single principle of justice, people should have recognized it; whereas in fact they disagree fundamentally. However, the same argument could be run against the principle of utility, something which Mill himself explicitly says people have not converged upon as the foundation of morality (1.1.12–14). He is perhaps led to make it because he believes that his argument for utilitarianism is scientifically respectable, and does not rely on appeal to self-evidence. In fact, however, he must so rely; see n. on 5.36.n. Mill's opponents will of course remain unimpressed by his argument here, since each will continue to insist that his principle of justice is correct, just as Mill insists that his principle of utility is correct. Moreover, when there are conflicts, the opponents will suggest, they are to be decided using the principle of justice. The argument also raises a question for Mill: if human beings have subliminally converged in the erection of a morality on the basis of their sentiments, why have they not converged on that single morality which will provide the best chance of security?

Paragraph 27

2 **no safety**: It is unclear what kind of safety Mill has in mind. If it is equivalent to security, then he himself has taken a position something like this. It is more likely to be epistemological 'safety', i.e. certainty.

11 **in the mind of one and the same individual**: This is of course not true of everyone. Someone of whom it is true may argue that there are indeed competing principles of justice, the precedence of which is to be judged in each particular case. Mill would respond that there must be one ultimate moral principle; see 1.3.31–5. To judge case by case is to be guided by one's own 'personal predilections'.

Paragraph 28

9 **Owen**: the British utopian socialist Robert Owen (1771–1858). Mill discusses Owen's determinism in *S* 8.839–42.

12 **All these opinions are extremely plausible**: Mill himself would have disagreed with the first and last, but not with the second.

13 **the principles which lie under justice**: Mill's opponent will argue that justice is foundational in itself.

17 **the acknowledged injustice**: But this is likely to be acknowledged only by those who accept the first position on justice; likewise the second principle of justice below.

21 **The Owenite invokes the admitted principle**: This principle is not in tension with the first two; what the Owenite rests his claim on is determinism, combined with this principle.

30 **the freedom of the will**: Mill himself believed that free action done from motives which were causally determined was possible; cf. *S* 8.836–7. The claim that the notion of the free will was dreamed up to justify punishment is pure fantasy.

35 **fiction of a contract**: Mill believed that social contract arguments were circular; see *S* 8.827.

41 *volenti non fit injuria*: See the *Digest* of Justinian, in Mommsen (1893: bk. 47, tit. 10, para. 1, sect. 5).

44 **this maxim**: i.e. the *volenti* principle.

47 **evidently came into use**: Mill seems to be imagining that the *volenti* principle was originally used to justify punishment. This is unlikely. For discussion of this principle, see Feinberg (1984: 115–17 and *passim*).

51 **not able to adhere consistently**: It could be said that courts are refining the principle in such cases, rather than setting it aside.

Paragraph 29

5 *lex talionis*: Latin, 'law of retaliation'. The most famous example is the biblical 'eye for an eye'; see Exod. 21.24; Matt. 5.38.

10 **how natural is the sentiment**: Mill's suggestion here is something of a hostage to fortune, since an opponent may argue that the naturalness of the sentiment suggests it has some objective ground; cf. 5.1.10–16.

17 **there are others to whom that consideration is all in all**: such as Mill himself. Mill could have stated this position more uncharitably, as the view that it is just to inflict any amount of suffering on a person if it is justified by the good it does overall.

Paragraph 31

16 **perceptions**: inserted in 3rd edn.

18 **a tacit influence**: another example of an assertion of subliminal moral psychology.

Paragraph 32

12 **certain classes of moral rules**: These are 'secondary principles', adherence to which is justified by the first principle of morality; see 2.24; 5.36; Introd., Sect. 6.

Paragraph 33

2 **wrongful interference**: Mill's account of what makes such interference wrongful is itself utilitarian; cf. *L* 18.224.
9 **every one would see in every one else a probable enemy**: cf. Hobbes's 'war of every man, against every man' (Hobbes 1651 / 1968: pt. 1, ch. 13); 'a probable enemy' replaced 'an enemy' in the 2nd edn.
13 **prudential instruction**: i.e. advice directed solely at the good of the other person.
   or think they gain: Because such help is virtuous, the pleasure in giving it is itself part of a person's own welfare; see 4.5–8.
17 **the moralities**: i.e. the moral principles.
32 **a physical or of a social ground**: Mill may be distinguishing here between expectations grounded in natural bonds (such as between a child and a parent) and those based on social institutions such as promising.

Paragraph 34

In the previous paragraph, Mill is concentrating on his first and second spheres of justice (legal and moral rights; see 5.5–6). He now moves to the third (desert; see 5.7), relating it at lines 11–23 to the fourth (breaking faith; see 5.8), which has already been itself connected to the first and second in 5.33.28–32.
22 **a sympathizing spectator**: See 2.18.5 and n.

Paragraph 36

Mill now returns to his final spheres of justice (see 5.9–10).
16 **this great moral duty rests upon a still deeper foundation**: Mill here fails to recognize the difference between treating people equally, and treating equal pleasures and pains equally. Utilitarianism could require great inequalities of treatment if utility would be maximized by so doing. Some awareness of the distinction may emerge in the footnote, where he objects to Spencer's view that utilitarianism requires that each person has an equal right to happiness. In the ordinary sense of 'equal right', this is quite incorrect. In the passage fol-

lowing the fn. reference Mill does appear to recognize the distinction, suggesting that people are to be treated equally *unless* such treatment fails to maximize utility.

23 **Bentham's dictum**: By this principle, Bentham meant that each pleasure and
each pain counted equally, regardless of who experienced them; cf. Bentham
(1789/1996: 1.4–7). The choice of the word 'dictum' (from *dicere*, Latin for 'to
say') may be deliberate: the phrase has not been found in any of Bentham's
writings.

25 **Herbert Spencer** (fn.): Mill is referring to Spencer (1851: 94). The letter to
Mill, with commentary by Spencer, is in Spencer (1904: vol. 2, 87–90).

guide to right (fn.): 'guide to be the foundation of right' in *Fraser's*.

the truths of arithmetic are applicable to the valuation of happiness (fn.):
This is perhaps the closest Mill comes to an explicit argument for utilitarianism. His claim is that the value of happiness increases according to
amount, with the implication that the greater the value the stronger the
reason to pursue it. Thus, what anyone has strongest reason to do is to maximize happiness ('truths of arithmetic' was 'rules of arithmetic' in *Fraser's*).

Mr Herbert Spencer, in a private communication . . . scientific proof (fn.):
In this paragraph added to the fn. in the 1st edn., Mill agrees with Spencer that
general reflection on the laws of human nature and of human life, as well as
empirical observation, are required to work out how best to maximize happiness. Mill goes on to suggest that these methods offer the possibility of scientific proof in ethics. Bentham is referred to frequently in the critique of the
'expediency-philosophy' in the *Social Statics* (Spencer 1851: 1–23). Mill believed
Bentham to have been the founder of ethics as a science: R 10.9–11.

48 **colour, race, and sex**: Mill does not here mention the tyranny of human
beings over non-human animals, though 2.10.14 implies that their utility is to
be counted in with that of human beings in utilitarian calculations. Because
animals do not experience higher pleasures, they will in fact matter little in
Mill's scheme of things except in so far as it may be important to prevent their
suffering. Mill says nothing about how higher and lower pleasures are to be
traded off against pains. For Mill's views on racism and sexism respectively, see
e.g. NQ (20.87–95) and SW (20.259–340).

Paragraph 37

4 **some other social duty**: Mill does not discuss the really difficult cases, in
which for example it would clearly maximize utility to kill or torture an innocent person. Here linguistic intuition tells against him: what utilitarianism
requires in such cases is injustice. Mill may have thought that such cases would
not arise in reality. For example, Mill believes that if during a siege the enemy
demand the surrender of some innocent person in return for calling off the
siege, the besiegers should not comply, for the sake of communal ties and

discouraging the attackers by their fortitude (Letter to W. T. Thornton (1863) 15.854). On exceptions to rules in general, see Letters to George Grote (1862) 15.762 and to E. W. Young (1867) 16.1327.

The discussion is anyway confusing, since Mill's earlier discussion of rights suggests that any duty to save a particular life will be an obligation of justice. What he needs is an example of a case in which a justice-based obligation is outweighed by a non-justice-based obligation. I may have promised to pay you back this evening the money I owe you, so that you have a right to expect repayment. But on my way I come across a beggar in dire need of money for food. I have no duty to help this beggar, since I have already done a great deal for beggars, but it could be that generosity trumps justice in this case.

Paragraph 38

3 **all cases of justice are also cases of expediency**: This phrase disguises the fact that, in some cases, following the secondary principles of justice will not maximize utility; rather it is this strategy taken as a whole which will maximize utility.

19 **sanctions**: cf. 3.1.2 and n.; Introd., Sect. 8.

Bibliography

ADAMS, R. M. (1976), 'Motive Utilitarianism', *Journal of Philosophy*, 73.

ARISTOTLE (1985; written *c*.330 BC), *Nicomachean Ethics*, trans. T. Irwin (Indianapolis).

BAIN, A. (1859), *The Emotions and the Will* (London).

BALES, R. E. (1971), 'Act Utilitarianism: Account of Right-Making Characteristics or Decision-Making Procedure?', *American Philosophical Quarterly*, 8.

BENTHAM, J. (1977; first pub. 1776), *A Fragment on Government*, ed. J. H. Burns and H. L. A. Hart (London).

——(1983), *Deontology*, ed. A. Goldworth (Oxford).

——(1996; first pub. 1789), *Introduction to the Principles of Morals and Legislation*, ed. J. H. Burns and H. L. A. Hart, introd. F. Rosen (Oxford).

BERGER, F. (1984), *Happiness, Justice, and Freedom* (Berkeley & Los Angeles).

BUTLER, J. (1897; first pub. 1726), *Works*, ed. W. E. Gladstone, 2 vols. (Oxford).

CARLYLE, T. (1836), *Sartor Resartus* (Boston).

——(1840), *Critical and Miscellaneous Essays*, 5 vols. (London).

COMTE, A. (1851–4), *Système de politique positive* (Paris).

CRISP, R. (1992), 'Utilitarianism and the Life of Virtue', *Philosophical Quarterly*, 42.

——(1997), *Mill on Utilitarianism* (London).

——and SLOTE, M. (eds.) (1997), *Virtue Ethics* (Oxford).

DAHL, N. O. (1973), 'Is Mill's Hedonism Inconsistent?', *American Philosophical Quarterly*, Monograph 7.

DAVIS, N. (1980), 'Utilitarianism and Responsibility', *Ratio*, 22.

DIOGENES LAERTIUS (1958; written *c*.230), *Lives of Eminent Philosophers*, trans. R. D. Hicks (London).

DRYER, D. P. (1969), 'Essay on Mill's *Utilitarianism*', introd. to J. S. Mill, *Collected Works*, vol. 10, ed. J. Robson (Toronto).

FARMER, D. H. (1992), *Oxford Dictionary of Saints*, 3rd edn. (Oxford).

FEINBERG, J. (1984), *Harm to Others* (New York).

GLARE, P. (ed.) (1982), *Oxford Latin Dictionary* (Oxford).

GLOVER, J. (1984), *What Sort of People Should There Be?* (Harmondsworth).

GREEN, T. H. (1883), *Prolegomena to Ethics* (Oxford).

GRIFFIN, J. (1982), 'Modern Utilitarianism', *Revue Internationale de Philosophie*, 141.

——(1986), *Well-Being* (Oxford).

HALL, E. R. (1949), 'The "Proof" of Utility in Bentham and Mill', *Ethics*, 60.

HARE, R. M. (1981), *Moral Thinking: Its Methods, Levels, and Point* (Oxford).

HARRIS, J. (1974), 'Williams on Negative Responsibility and Integrity', *Philosophical Quarterly*, 24.

Bibliography

HARTLEY, D. (1749), *Observations on Man, His Frame, His Duty, and His Expectations*, 2 vols. (London).

HOBBES, T. (1968; first pub. 1651), *Leviathan*, ed. C. B. Macpherson (Harmondsworth).

HOLLIS, M. (1995), 'The Shape of a Life', in J. Altham and R. Harrison (eds.), *World, Mind, and Ethics* (Cambridge).

HOOKER, B. (1995), 'Rule-Consequentialism, Incoherence, Fairness', *Proceedings of the Aristotelian Society*, 95.

HUME, D. (1975; first pub. 1751), *An Enquiry concerning the Principles of Morals*, ed. L. Selby-Bigge, 3rd edn., rev. P. H. Nidditch (Oxford).

——(1978; first pub. 1739–40), *A Treatise of Human Nature*, ed. L. Selby-Bigge, 2nd edn., rev. P. H. Nidditch (Oxford).

KANT, I. (1950; first pub. 1787, 2nd edn.), *Critique of Pure Reason*, trans. N. Kemp Smith (London).

——(1995; first pub. 1785), *Foundations of the Metaphysics of Morals*, trans. L. W. Beck, 2nd edn. (Upper Saddle River, NJ).

——(1996), *Practical Philosophy*, trans. and ed. M. Gregor (Cambridge).

LOCKE, J. (1975; first pub. 1690), *An Essay Concerning Human Understanding*, ed. P. H. Nidditch (Oxford).

LONG, A. and SEDLEY, D. (1987), *The Hellenistic Philosophers*, vol. 1 (Cambridge).

LYONS, D. (1965), *The Forms and Limits of Utilitarianism* (Oxford).

——(1994), *Rights, Welfare, and Mill's Moral Theory* (Oxford).

MARTIN, R. (1972), 'A Defence of Mill's Qualitative Hedonism', *Philosophy*, 47.

MARX, K. (1964), *The German Ideology*, trans. and ed. S. Ryazanskaya (Moscow).

McCLOSKEY, H. J. (1957), 'An Examination of Restricted Utilitarianism', *Philosophical Review*, 66.

MILL, JAMES (1829), *Analysis of the Phenomena of the Human Mind* (London).

——(1835), *A Fragment on Mackintosh* (London).

MOMMSEN, T. (ed.) (1893), *Corpus Iuris Civilis*, vol. 1 (Berlin).

MOORE, G. E. (1903), *Principia Ethica* (Cambridge).

MURRAY, J. A. H., BRADLEY, H., CRAIGIE, W. A., and ONIONS, C. T. (eds.) (1928), *Oxford English Dictionary*, vol. 10, pt. 2.

NIETZSCHE, F. (1966; first pub. 1886), *Beyond Good and Evil*, trans. W. Kaufman (New York).

NOZICK, R. (1974), *Anarchy, State, and Utopia* (Oxford).

O'NEILL, O. (1991), 'Kantian Ethics', in P. Singer (ed.), *A Companion to Ethics* (Oxford).

PACKE, M. (1954), *The Life of John Stuart Mill* (London).

PALEY, W. (1785), *Principles of Moral and Political Philosophy* (London).

PARFIT, D. (1984), *Reasons and Persons* (Oxford).

PLATO (1976; written c.390 BC), *Protagoras*, trans. C. C. W. Taylor (Oxford).

——(1979; written c.385 BC), *Gorgias*, trans. T. Irwin (Oxford).

Bibliography

——(1992; written *c.*380 BC), *Republic*, trans. G. M. A. Grube, rev. C. D. C. Reeve (Indianapolis).

PRIOR, A. N. (1949), *Logic and the Basis of Ethics* (Oxford).

PUTNAM, H. (1981), *Reason, Truth, and History* (Cambridge).

RACHELS, J. (1991), 'Subjectivism', in P. Singer (ed.), *A Companion to Ethics* (Oxford).

RAILTON, P. (1984), 'Alienation, Consequentialism, and the Demands of Morality', *Philosophy and Public Affairs*, 13.

RYAN, A. (1970), *The Philosophy of John Stuart Mill* (London).

——(1974), *J. S. Mill* (London).

——(ed.) (1993), *Justice* (Oxford).

SCHEFFLER, S. (ed.) (1988), *Consequentialism and its Critics* (Oxford).

SETH, J. (1908), 'The Alleged Fallacies in Mill's "Utilitarianism"', *Philosophical Review*, 17.

SIDGWICK, H. (1907), *The Methods of Ethics*, 7th edn. (London).

SINNOTT-ARMSTRONG, W. and TIMMONS, M. (eds.) (1996), *Moral Knowledge?* (New York).

SKORUPSKI, J. (1989), *John Stuart Mill* (London).

SMITH, A. (1976; first pub. 1759), *A Theory of the Moral Sentiments*, ed. D. D. Raphael and A. L. Macfie (Oxford).

SPENCER, H. (1851), *Social Statics* (London).

——(1904), *Autobiography*, 2 vols. (London).

SUMNER, L. W. (1992), 'Welfare, Happiness, and Pleasure', *Utilitas*, 4.

URMSON, J. O. (1953), 'The Interpretation of the Moral Philosophy of J. S. Mill', *Philosophical Quarterly*, 3.

WEST, H. R. (1976), 'Mill's Qualitative Hedonism', *Philosophy*, 51.

WHEWELL, W. (1837), *On the Foundations of Morals*, 2nd edn. (Cambridge).

——(1845), *The Elements of Morality*, 2 vols. (London).

WIDHAGEN, K. and HÉRANCOURT, W. (eds.) (1972), *English-German German-English Dictionary*, 2 vols. (Wiesbaden).

WILLIAMS, B. (1973), 'A Critique of Utilitarianism', in J. Smart and B. Williams, *Utilitarianism For and Against* (Cambridge).

——(1985), *Ethics and the Limits of Philosophy* (London).

WITTGENSTEIN, L. (1958), *Philosophical Investigations*, trans. G. E. M. Anscombe (Oxford).

Index

Index